The RFU Guide for Coaches Fitness and Conditioning

Ian Taplin

RUGBY
FOOTBALL
UNION

A&C Black • London

Published in 2005 by
A & C Black Publishers Ltd
37 Soho Square, London W1D 3QZ
www.acblack.com

Copyright © 2005 by the RFU

ISBN 0 7136 7179 3

A CIP catalogue record for this book
is available from the British Library.

A & C Black uses paper produced with elemental chlorine-
free pulp, harvested from managed sustainable forests.

Acknowledgments
Cover photograph © Actionplus
Photograph on p. 171 © Getty Images.
All other textual photographs by Guy Hearn
Cover and inside design by James Watson

This book has been typeset in Goudy

Printed and bound in Great Britain by
Biddles Ltd, King's Lynn

Contents

Foreword

Any coach who can increase the fitness levels of his or her players will achieve a dramatic improvement in individual and team performance. As such, knowledge about fitness and the part it plays in producing winning teams has always been high on the shopping list of ambitious coaches. It is strange, then, that there is such a dearth of appropriate books, papers, DVDs and other information on the subject. This book attempts to fill that void and provide solutions for the coach who seeks to bring players to match day in peak condition.

The changing nature of the game, where the ball is in play for far longer periods and for a larger proportion of total playing time than ever before, means that to contribute effectively to the game, players have to be markedly fitter than their predecessors. Indeed, the commonly used term of 'athlete' conveys to player and spectator alike what is expected in the modern game. The RFU, like many other leading governing bodies, has initiated a Long Term Athlete Development programme (LTAD), founded on principles promoted by Istvan Bayli, to ensure they have a 'big picture' view of the development of players; their physical wellbeing is at the forefront of this.

This book is not aimed solely at coaches; while much can rest on the coach's shoulders, players are being encouraged more and more to take on responsibility for their own fitness levels. The RFU Coach Education programme confirms the need to develop all-round healthy lifestyles as well as improved generic and position-specific fitness levels; this will enhance what a player can give to the game and hence increase enjoyment through extended participation.

Throughout this book, basic information is expanded in box format to give greater insight, terminology is clearly explained and there are many references to direct the reader to more in-depth knowledge about a particular topic. So, whether you are a player, coach, trainer or fitness expert, this book will have something to offer. Integrate conditioning into your sessions to gain maximum benefit; start your season with a team you can be proud of; keep going through the rigours of the winter months and come to the end of the season knowing that your team was not found wanting on the fitness front.

Des Diamond
RFU Coaching Development Manager

Acknowledgements

There are a number of people whose support and contributions have made this book possible. Thank you in particular to Michelle Cuthbert, Kate Arthur, Richard Horner and Alan Pearson (SAQ International) for their expertise and input into a number of chapters. A special thanks goes to Jan Bonney, Matt Hart, Owen Gregory, Tom Stokes, Ruth Barton, Amy Turner and Michaela Staniford for their modelling in the photoshoot. Thank you also to Andy Maren, Martin Knights and the players and management at Richmond FC for their assistance and for allowing me to trial many of the activities that make up this book. Most importantly, thank you to my wife Kate, whose support and understanding has been an inspiration throughout.

Introduction

At the elite level rugby players are finely-tuned athletes whose training is meticulously planned to ensure that physically, mentally and tactically they are able to perform to their full ability. In the amateur game players obviously do not have the same time and opportunity to develop their athletic and rugby potential, although many players will still train five to six times a week despite having the demands of a full-time job. As a coach it is vital that this commitment is maximised by providing advice and training sessions that bring about improvements in the player and athlete.

The resources available to the coach to develop their understanding of the technical and tactical areas of the game are vast. However, there is little to support them with regards to the development of physical fitness and conditioning for rugby. The aim of this book is to provide support to the coach in this increasingly significant area of the game.

This book is for coaches and players at all levels who want to gain a better understanding of the role that fitness plays in rugby. The scientific principles of training will be explained and then applied in a rugby setting to demonstrate how they are relevant to the sport. There is a difference between being physically 'fit', and being conditioned for the demands of a high-impact game like rugby. The functional needs of the sport will be addressed and exercises and drills provided that will enable the maximum transfer of benefit from training to performance.

Fitness for rugby

Since the advent of the professional era, rugby has made great strides at all levels in terms of improving the organisation, structure and specificity of fitness training. In regards to the England international squad, the improvements in physical training and conditioning have played a major factor in England's ability to play an expansive, high-intensity game for the whole 80 minutes.

Scientific research supports what is obvious to anyone watching international rugby, that players are bigger, faster and stronger, can run all day and move with a grace and dynamism which belies their increased mass. Of course this has not happened by chance, but rather through a systematic, deliberate fitness regime and a new philosophy towards this aspect of the game. This is most poignantly illustrated by the subtle change in the way members of the England squad are regarded – they are no longer merely players, but athletes. The average weight of an England international player has increased by 10 kg in only 20 years, and match time and actual playing time have also increased dramatically by over 40 per cent since the 1991 Rugby World Cup, with the ball in play for on average an extra seven minutes in the 2003 Six Nations.

The more junior levels of the game have also witnessed an improvement in the athletic ability of players. This is due to better facilities (mainly weights rooms), improved coach education and in some cases hiring specialist fitness advisors.

While coaches may recognise the need to have a planned fitness programme, in many cases it only lasts until competitive fixtures begin. Constraints on coach-to-player contact time and the need to concentrate on tactical aspects of the game often come at the expense of conditioning.

Components of fitness

Before you can begin developing your fitness, it is first important to understand what the components of fitness are, and how they are applied in rugby.

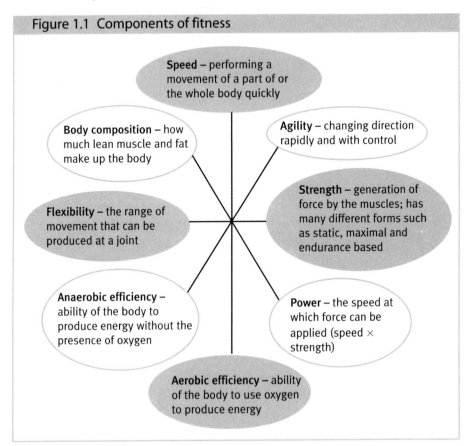

Figure 1.1 Components of fitness

Speed – performing a movement of a part of or the whole body quickly

Agility – changing direction rapidly and with control

Body composition – how much lean muscle and fat make up the body

Strength – generation of force by the muscles; has many different forms such as static, maximal and endurance based

Flexibility – the range of movement that can be produced at a joint

Anaerobic efficiency – ability of the body to produce energy without the presence of oxygen

Power – the speed at which force can be applied (speed × strength)

Aerobic efficiency – ability of the body to use oxygen to produce energy

All of the physical components in the diagram opposite play a major role in successful performance and need to be developed accordingly. To understand how these components are relevant, you need to look at rugby and analyse the movements and actions that make up the sport. All of the above components of fitness will be looked at in greater detail later on in this book. Now we are going to focus on aerobic and anaerobic fitness and how these are relevant to rugby.

Principles of training

The principles of training need to be adhered to in order for improvements to be made. These principles apply to all athletes; following them will result in greater advances in athletic performance, more relevant training and less time away from the game due to injury.

Assessment and suitability

Players should be assessed by the club physiotherapist and a detailed injury history compiled so that specific preventative work can be implemented as appropriate. Mobility and other assessments should be carried out to determine an individual's suitability to perform certain exercises and training methods.

Goal setting and testing

Players should have relevant physical testing carried out so strengths and weaknesses can be assessed. From this a training programme can be developed to best meet the player's needs.

Overload

For training improvements to occur the body must be challenged and worked at a level to which it is not accustomed. This overload needs to be carefully monitored and be planned with periods of rest (tapering) in order to prevent overtraining.

Specificity

Training should be as specific as possible to reflect the physical demands of the sport, position and individual needs.

Reversibility

If the system of overload is not followed then further gains will not be made. If training ceases then the gains and the adaptations from training are quickly lost.

Frequency and type

In order to bring about significant improvements a programme of regular training needs to be undertaken and continued. The frequency and type of training needs to reflect the stages of the periodised year.

Recovery

This is possibly the most important principle – time must be allowed when training and between sessions for the body to recover, and for physical adaptations to take place.

What happens in a game?

The game is made up of short periods of intermittent sprinting, wrestling and explosive collisions with varying lengths of rest separating this intense activity. The ability to recover and perform these activities is the key to rugby fitness.

As a game can last for nearly an hour and a half many people mistakenly believe that aerobic fitness is the most important training requirement. The game may last in excess of 80 minutes but it is dominated by power, strength and speed, with the average passage of play lasting only 15 minutes. Activities such as tackling and sprinting require energy more quickly and in greater amounts than can be produced by the aerobic system. Players may work at a high intensity for a few seconds, mauling for the ball, and then work at a low intensity for a minute, walking to a line-out. The ability for players to carry out this high-intensity work is dependent upon their anaerobic efficiency and it is this type of training that offers the most benefit in terms of rugby-specific fitness. The aerobic system does, however, need to be developed as it is during these rest periods that oxygen is used to replenish the energy stores, enabling a player to carry out further high-intensity effort.

Listed below are some of the actions that players will perform during a game – low-intensity efforts will take up the vast majority of game time as the ball is generally in play for only a third of the time. The time the ball is not in play should be viewed as recovery time; this can range from a few seconds to a few minutes if a try is scored or an injury has occurred. The average period when the ball is not in play is around 30 seconds. Training activities should reflect the recovery and activity periods that players will encounter in matches.

The time the ball is in play can range from anywhere between a few seconds to a couple of minutes. This will involve a mix of low- and high-intensity efforts, and it is the body's ability to cope and recover that enables this multi-phase rugby to be played.

Low-intensity effort
- Standing
- Walking
- Jogging

High-intensity effort
- Rucking
- Mauling
- Sprinting
- Scrummaging
- Supporting
- Tackling
- Ball carries in contact

Forwards will generally carry out more high-intensity efforts than backs through the course of a game, which tend to be more contact- than sprint-based. Backs may perform fewer efforts, but they will involve more sprinting and greater recovery time between bouts of activity. Though the ball may be in play, backs can be performing low-intensity activity when the ball is in a line-out, scrum or maul, in which they are generally less involved.

At the highest level there are a number of sophisticated tracking programmes that are used to monitor individual effort levels during matches and the recovery time between these efforts. This is used to understand the demands that the modern game places on players and is then used to devise training programmes to reflect this most accurately. This has shown that the anaerobic systems are the most desired means of energy production in rugby. Both forwards and backs need to be able to work for a few seconds at maximal effort and be able to produce sustained high-intensity effort for 30–40 seconds if required. Though there are position-specific differences in the type of work carried out, anaerobic training can be manipulated with different effort, rest and activity type to meet the positional demands.

It is important that an aerobic base is developed in order to meet the energy demands through the course of a game. The aerobic system needs to be sufficiently developed to deal with waste products and replenish energy supplies, otherwise fatigue will set in and players will be unable to meet the energy demands that are required.

Energy production for rugby

The body's demand for energy is supplied by ATP (Adenosine Tri-Phosphate), which is available in limited supplies with only enough for a few seconds of maximal effort before it is exhausted. ATP is constantly being made (re-synthesised) to ensure that energy needs can be met. In order to do so ATP can be re-synthesised in different ways and at different speeds. This occurs most rapidly through the anaerobic pathway and more gradually through the aerobic.

The energy systems do not work in isolation; they are all supplying energy at the same time but in different amounts depending on the demand for energy. The more intense the activity the greater the role of the anaerobic systems, while lower intensity, longer duration exercise is more reliant on the aerobic system.

Anaerobic energy production

The anaerobic energy pathway has two routes and produces energy without using oxygen:

ATP-PC system (alactic system)

This uses a substance called phosphocreatine to create ATP. Like ATP this is only available in limited amounts, can only produce energy for a few seconds of effort and is quickly exhausted. This system is used to produce energy quickly and when a great deal of force is required (when sprinting and jumping, for example).

Anaerobic glycolysis (lactic system)

This uses the body's glycogen stores (from our diet) to produce ATP that can be used for energy production. It does not produce ATP and thus energy as quickly as the PC system, and is not as effective as a form of energy for maximal efforts. It does, however, enable high-intensity activity to be maintained for a considerable period by providing energy in large amounts (the first two minutes of energy production are dominated by the anaerobic system) before the by-product of the system, lactic acid, prevents further ATP re-synthesis.

Aerobic energy production

Oxygen is used to facilitate the re-synthesis of ATP; this is a slower process and as such is not as effective in producing explosive movements, although it does produce large amounts of ATP and provides energy for longer duration events. During rest periods in a game it is the aerobic system that is responsible for replenishing ATP (energy) stores and enabling maximal or high-intensity effort to be resumed.

All players need to train in a way that targets and stresses the anaerobic energy systems, increasing tolerance to fatigue and increasing the rate at which these systems recover and are ready to provide energy again.

Table 1.1 Energy sources in rugby

Intensity and time of effort	Maximal – 5 to 10 seconds	Mixed – 10 to 60 seconds	Mixed – 60 seconds plus	Maximal – 5 to 10 seconds	Mixed – 10 to 60 seconds	Mixed – 60 seconds plus
Recovery between efforts	60 seconds plus	20 to 60 seconds	20 to 60 seconds	60 seconds or less	60 seconds plus	60 seconds plus
Main energy source	ATP-PC	Anaerobic glycolysis	Anaerobic glycolysis/aerobic	Anaerobic glycolysis	Anaerobic glycolysis	Anaerobic glycolysis/aerobic
Why?	Short duration activity and sufficient time for replenishment of PC stores in the recovery period.	ATP-PC source will not be able to meet prolonged energy demand or recover sufficiently in the limited rest period to produce the main energy supply for the next phase of activity.	The limited recovery period between two long periods of effort will tax the anaerobic system to its limits. As a result the aerobic system will be required to provide a significant amount of energy to perform the activity. Particularly for forwards whose involvement in the phases of play will be more active than backs.	ATP-PC source will not have recovered sufficiently in the limited rest period to provide the main energy supply for the next effort, though it will play a significant role.	ATP-PC source will not be able to meet prolonged energy demand. Will have recovered sufficiently to be dominant in early stages but then will be taken over by the anaerobic system.	Anaerobic glycolysis will still be the dominant energy source but the aerobic system will play a more significant role as the time increases, particularly for forwards whose involvement in the phases of play will be more active than backs.

As with the core technical skills that rugby players require, they need to have a degree of competence in the physical components of fitness required for rugby. Once this has been established, a more personalised and position-specific approach can be taken to develop the areas of most relevance to the individual.

Forwards and backs – basic training differences

Forwards will hit more rucks and mauls and effect more tackles, generally being more actively involved in a passage of play for longer in comparison to backs. As such, their training needs to be based more around the anaerobic lactic system.

Backs require a sound anaerobic base but will perform fewer efforts, which are predominately sprint-based and with longer recovery periods. Thus the PC system and speed development will play a greater role for backs than it would for forwards.

Game 'based' conditioning

Having established how the energy systems function during a game it is important to tailor training to reflect these requirements, hence game 'based' conditioning. This means that the effort and recovery time, the type and intensity of the activity and the energy systems used are stressed as closely as possible 'based' on the conditions that occur during a game.

This type of training will involve sprinting (multi-directional), jumping, wrestling, ball skills, tackling, rucking, mauling, down and ups, and other rugby-based movements. This form of training is highly specific to the demands of the game and work/rest times can be altered to target a particular energy system to a greater degree. This will bring about improvements in the functioning capacity of all three energy systems, but will particularly improve the body's ability to work anaerobically, developing greater tolerance to lactic acid and working at a higher intensity for longer.

Aerobic training

Before embarking on game-based training, players do require a base level of aerobic fitness to enable recovery to be rapid and to perform for the duration of the game. Traditional aerobic base development involved long, steady, continuous activity, but this is not particularly specific to rugby. Fartlek, interval and circuit training are a much more effective way of developing the endurance base required for rugby. By reducing the time but increasing/varying the intensity of the effort (60–80 per cent) the aerobic system is still dominant in energy production but the lactic system is also recruited to a greater extent.

Players with a well-developed level of aerobic fitness will be able to perform a greater number of high-intensity efforts in a game, due to the speed of recovery and its involvement in energy production during long passages of play. This aerobic base should be developed in the pre-season and then gradually replaced by more anaerobic game-based conditioning as the season approaches. Players who are returning from injury or who have high levels of body fat may need to revisit this type of training depending on their specific training status.

Below are some sample sessions that will help to develop this aerobic base and enable a more rapid progression to the more specific game-based conditioning.

Anaerobic threshold

This is the point when the aerobic energy system cannot satisfy the body's energy demands sufficiently, so the body becomes increasingly dependent on the anaerobic systems.

Developing the aerobic base

Four-minute intervals

This form of interval training will predominately develop the aerobic system, but because of the intensity of effort there will also be considerable benefits to the lactic system. This is because players should be working around their anaerobic threshold, and in order to maintain running speed the anaerobic system has to be recruited more than with steady, long-duration training.

Description:
1. Perform the sets as detailed in table 1.2.
2. Players run for four minutes and try to achieve as great a distance as possible.
3. Drop-off in distances between the sets should be minimal and pace needs to be judged accordingly to achieve this.

Perform on a track or pitch and record the distances covered.

Table 1.2 Four-minute intervals

Position	Target distance/ 4 minutes	Rep 1 metres	Rep 2 metres	Rep 3 metres	Rep 4 metres	Rep 5 metres
Front five	600–1000					
Back row	800–1200					
Inside backs	800–1200					
Outside backs	700–1100					

Reps: 3–5 with 2 minutes walking and jogging recovery.

Sets: 1

Variations: Start with 3 reps and increase by 1 rep every 3 sessions until you are performing 5 reps.

Reduce the recovery time but maintain the distance covered.

Increase the recovery time and increase the distance covered.

The training session described above can be adapted and performed on a rowing machine, bike or stepper. Though not as rugby-specific, they do provide an excellent workout and may be highly appropriate for forwards in particular as they are not weight bearing. This will reduce the strain on the joints that running can have for players who are carrying a lot of weight.

Pyramid interval rowing

Rowing is an excellent all-round exercise and will develop the aerobic and the lactic systems. Recovery time is kept low to stress the aerobic system and to keep the players working around the anaerobic threshold.

Description:
1. Perform the rows as detailed in table 1.3 below completing the prescribed distance and observing the recovery times.
2. Work at an intensity that produces a limited drop-off in the distances covered.

Table 1.3 Distances and recovery times for pyramid interval rowing

Distance	Recovery time
1000 m	1 min
500 m	30 sec
500 m	30 sec
1000 m	End

Sets: Perform 2 sets of the above intervals with 4 minutes recovery between sets.

Variations: Increasing the recovery times will enable a higher intensity of effort and make the exercise more anaerobic.

The principles that are applied to the following running-based interval, fartlek and pyramid drills can all be utilised on a rowing machine.

Yo-yo pyramid interval

This form of interval training will develop the aerobic and the lactic system. The short recovery times and varying distances mean that both systems are heavily stressed.

Description:

Perform on a track or on a rugby pitch (try line to try line represents approx. 100 m).

1. Perform the activities described in table 1.4 below with the prescribed rest and recovery periods.
2. Keep the intensity as high as possible throughout.
3. Record the times taken for each run and try and maintain these for the corresponding run that follows later in the set. The difference between the first and last 400-metre run should be as little as possible.

Table 1.4 Distances and recovery times for yo-yo pyramid interval

Distance	Recovery time
400 m	45 seconds
300 m	45 seconds
200 m	30 seconds
200 m	30 seconds
300 m	45 seconds
400 m	End of set

Sets: 3 minutes recovery then repeat set.

Variations: Reduce the recovery time but maintain the distance covered. Increase the recovery time and increase the distance covered.

200-metre interval runs

This form of interval training will develop the aerobic and the lactic systems. The medium recovery times will allow for partial recovery of the anaerobic system and thus the aerobic system has a prominent role to play.

Description:
Perform on a track or on a rugby pitch.

1. Perform the activities described below with the prescribed rest and recovery periods.
2. Keep the intensity as high as possible throughout.
3. Record the times taken for each run and try and maintain these. The difference between the first and last runs should be as slight as possible and with a good speed maintained on all the other runs.
4. Start by performing 1 or 2 sets of 6 repetitions depending on the level of fitness. Add an extra repetition each week until you are performing 2 sets of 10 repetitions.

Reps: 6–10 × 200 m with 30 seconds recovery between each run.

Sets: 1–2 with 3 minutes rest between sets.

Variations: Increase the recovery time between runs and raise the intensity of effort accordingly. Perform 1 set of 6 repetitions only. This will make the exercise more anaerobic and develop speed endurance.

Fartlek

Fartlek training will develop the aerobic and the lactic systems in a manner that closely reflects the demands of a game. Effort is continuous but the intensity is varied, which requires the anaerobic and aerobic systems to supplement each other in order to work at the required intensity.

Description:
Perform the runs as detailed in table 1.5, working to the required intensity and distance. Work from try line to try line (approx. 100 m) to judge the distance covered.

Sets: 2–3 with 2 minutes rest between sets.

Variations: Adjust the distance run and intensity of effort to stress the energy systems in different ways. More rugby-based movements can be added to make the exercise more specific and anaerobic.

Table 1.5 Intensity levels for fartlek training

Distance	Intensity of run
400 m	70%
150 m	80%
50 m	90%
100 m	70%
20 m	Walk
300 m	70%
20 m	Walk
100 m	70%
50 m	90%
150 m	80%
400 m	70%
1 min jog/walk	

Anaerobic training

This form of game-based conditioning will predominately work the anaerobic systems by increasing the intensity of the effort to 80–100 per cent of maximal effort. The recovery time, work period and intensity will determine the extent to which the ATP-PC system or the lactic system is targeted. By training the ATP-PC system speed and power developments will be enhanced. Recovery and lactic tolerance will be improved by developing the lactic system and generally improving the capacity to work anaerobically. As the intensity and duration of the exercise increases, the aerobic system will be called upon to contribute an increasing amount of energy as the anaerobic system begins to tire.

Developing the anaerobic base

All of the following drills are designed to be included in club training sessions or performed as part of an individual programme. When performing this type of training the intensity needs to be high, but each repetition should be completed in a similar time to maintain the intensity and quality of effort. Players should pace themselves so that they work at a high intensity when performing the repetitions; the drop-off between the first and last repetition in each set should be minimal.

Training tip

By varying the length of recovery time between reps and sets, the focus of training can be manipulated to target an energy system more closely. Mixing the length of recovery times during a drill will make it highly specific, reflecting the varied nature of recovery times in rugby. The same principle can be applied to work times by performing double repetitions of the exercise to increase the work time. The table on page 7 detailing the use of energy systems in rugby will help you to determine these work/rest times.

The following two drills will stress the anaerobic systems by using work ratios that are commonly experienced during a game; the rest periods are kept high to allow for a greater intensity of effort. The aerobic system will become more actively involved with energy production as fatigue sets in and will also help players to recover between runs.

Interval run

Description:
1. Perform the activities described below with the prescribed rest and recovery periods.
2. Keep the intensity as high as possible throughout.

Set: 2×120 m at 80–90 per cent (jog back recovery and 2 minutes rest between runs).

         3×100 m at 80–90 per cent (jog back recovery and $1\frac{1}{2}$ minutes rest between runs).

         4×80 m at 80–90 per cent (jog back recovery and 1 minute rest between runs).

4 minutes rest and repeat the set.

Variations: Perform the intervals the opposite way around.

High to low interval pyramid

Description:
1. Perform the activities described below with the prescribed rest and recovery periods.
2. Keep the intensity as high as possible throughout.

Set: 4×150 m at $80+$ per cent – try line to try line and then to halfway line (jog back recovery and 90 seconds rest).
4×120 m at $80+$ per cent – try line to try line and then to 22-metre line (jog back recovery and 90 seconds rest).
4×80 m at $80+$ per cent – try line to far 22-metre line (jog back recovery and 60 seconds rest).
4×50 m at $80+$ per cent – try line to halfway line (jog back recovery and 60 seconds rest).

Perform 1 set only.

Record or set target times so players can gauge their level of effort throughout the exercise.

Variations: Carry out the pyramid the opposite way around, low to high.

The next two drills will stress the anaerobic systems by using work and rest ratios that are commonly experienced during a game and with rugby-based movements. The aerobic system will become more actively involved with energy production as fatigue sets in and will also help players to recover between sets.

Mixed distance intervals

Description:
1. Perform the activities described below with the prescribed rest and recovery periods.
2. Keep the intensity as high as possible throughout.

Set 1: 3×150 m – try line to try line and back to halfway.
90 seconds recovery between reps.
2 minutes rest before next set.

Set 2: 8×22 m – try line to 22-metre line.
20 seconds recovery between reps.
60 seconds rest before next set.

Set 3: 4×100 m – try line to try line.
60 seconds recovery between reps.
2 minutes rest before next set.

Set 4: 6×50 m – try line to halfway line.
30 seconds recovery between reps.

Variations: Utilise different start positions, get-ups and rolling, multi-directional starts, especially for the shorter runs.

Mixed activity intervals

Description:

1. Perform the activities described below with the prescribed rest and recovery periods.
2. Keep the intensity as high as possible throughout.

Activity 1: 3 × 200 m – try line to try line and back.
60 seconds recovery between reps.
2 minutes rest before next activity.

Activity 2: In pairs, 6 reps × 3 sets of shield drives (see Fig. 1.2) going down and up at the cones before completing a drive. Stress technique and getting up quickly.
20 seconds recovery between sets (while partner is working).
45 seconds rest before next activity.

Figure 1.2 Shield drives

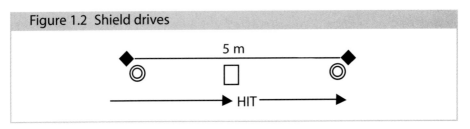

Activity 3: In pairs, 5-second wrestles into a 120-metre run.
4 × wrestle and 120 m – try line to try line and to 22-metre line nearest to second try line.
60 seconds recovery between reps.
2 minutes rest before next activity.

Activity 4: 6 × 30-metre agility run (see Fig. 1.3) – dead ball line to 22-metre line.
45 seconds recovery between reps.

Figure 1.3 30-metre agility run

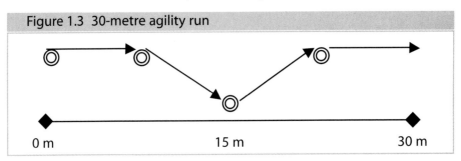

Variations: Use different distances and rugby-based activities.

Powerbag throw and run

This drill involves dynamic throwing and getting up off the floor as quickly as possible. This will stress the anaerobic systems by using work and rest ratios that are commonly experienced during a game; the aerobic system will be used to promote recovery.

Description:

1. Player performs three throws from the chest, going down and up after each one.
2. The player then gets up and runs forwards around the first cone/pole and backwards to the start.
3. Next, the player goes down so the chest is on the floor, then gets up using rebound technique and runs forwards and around the second cone/pole and runs forwards back to the start.

Figure 1.4 Powerbag throw and run

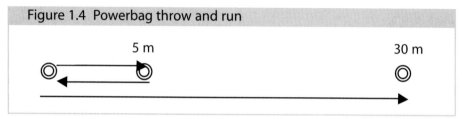

5 m   30 m

Reps: Player performs 6 runs with 30–60 seconds recovery between runs.

Sets: 1–2 depending on fitness level with 2 minutes recovery between sets.

Variations: Substitute the powerbag throws for tackle bag – tackle and throw.

Wrestling and rugby

Rugby is essentially made up of running- and wrestling-type activities, mauling, tackling and competing for the ball. Wrestling-type activities should form a large part of game-based fitness and provide an activity that is highly specific to rugby.

Wrestling activities

Ground work

Make a tackle and get up quickly, pushing off the tackled man/ball, and immediately try to win the ball. The player on the floor resists for the allotted time before reversing roles. The

player on the floor can lie on his side to reflect the position in which tacklers often have to work to steal the ball.

Ball wrestle

Drive a tackle shield held by your partner, who then drops the shield and picks up a ball, which the players wrestle over for the allotted time.

Swim wrestle

Players work in pairs and hug with one arm over their partner's shoulder and the other under. Both players attempt to bring the arm that is above their partner's shoulder under their partner's shoulder while trying to prevent their partner achieving this. Work for the allotted time.

Wrestle and run

This is a partner drill that involves an initial wrestling activity to simulate a contest for the ball and then a race against each other around the coned course. This is a good exercise for developing core and rugby-specific strength, and will stress the anaerobic systems by using work and rest ratios that are commonly experienced during a game; the aerobic system will be used to promote recovery.

Description:
1. Players wrestle for control of a ball in pairs for 15 seconds.
2. The coach times this and signals the end of the wrestle and the players then sprint around the coned course in their lanes, racing against each other.
3. At the far cone the players perform a down and up, and race back to the start.

Reps: 6 runs with 30–60 seconds recovery between runs.

Sets: 1–2 depending on fitness level with 2 minutes recovery between sets.

Variations: Increase work times (distance) and vary rest–time ratio. Wrestle for control of the ball at the end of the allocated time.
Add shield clear or tackle bags to run section at the turn.

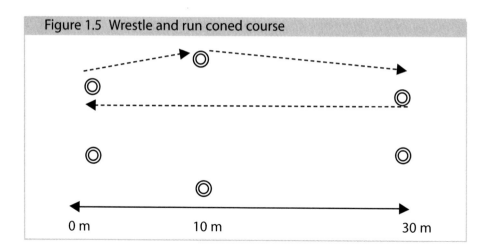

Figure 1.5 Wrestle and run coned course

0 m   10 m   30 m

Wrestle and clear

This is a partner drill that involves an initial wrestling activity to simulate a contest for the ball, and then high-intensity defensive work where communication and technique should be stressed.

Description:
Groups of 16 (8 working, 8 holding shields).

1. Wrestle in pairs for 5 seconds.
2. Then all 8 players line up and clear/drive shield carriers.
3. Run to opposite cone and go down onto chest after clearing shield (4 clears per set).

Communication and correct technique should be maintained.

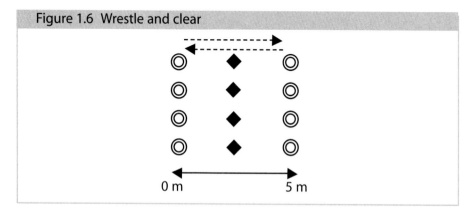

Figure 1.6 Wrestle and clear

0 m   5 m

Reps: Perform 4–6 repetitions with recovery time being the work time of the other group.

Sets: 1–2 sets depending on fitness level with 2 minutes recovery between sets.

Variations: Use pyramid work times and vary rest–time ratio.

Wrestle for control of the ball at the end of the allocated time.

Replace the shield with a tackle bag.

Add passing or decision making after clearing the shields.

Wrestle, run and clear

This is a partner drill that involves an initial wrestling activity to simulate a contest for the ball and then high-intensity running and physical contact.

Description:

Groups of 4 (2 working, 2 holding shields). Work in pairs of similar fitness levels.

1. Wrestle in pairs for 10 seconds.
2. Race each other over 30-metre loop performing down and ups, then clear/drive shield at 2 points (A and B).
3. Perform a down and up at the turn of the 30-metre loop.
4. When players have completed their set, swap with a shield man who repeats the set.
5. If performing more than 1 rep, when returning to the start position immediately resume wrestling and complete the course as before.

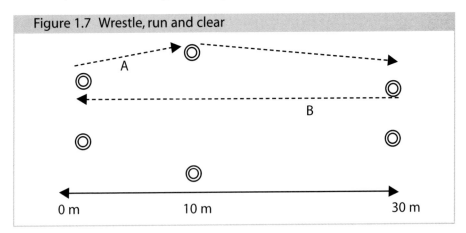

Figure 1.7 Wrestle, run and clear

Reps: As in table 1.6 opposite.

Sets: Perform the exercise as described in table 1.6. Allow 3–4 minutes recovery if performing this more than once.

Variations: Wrestle for control of the ball at the end of the allocated time.

Use tackle bags instead of shields in run section.

Table 1.6 Sets and reps for wrestle, run and clear

Set	Reps	Recovery Time
1	1	While other pairs are working (approx. 40–90 seconds depending on set)
2	2	
3	1	
4	3	
5	1	
6	1	

The next two drills are highly rugby-specific and involve actions that players will frequently use during a game. The intensity should be high to stress the anaerobic systems, with a good recovery period to ensure that the intensity can be maintained throughout the exercise.

Fitness 4s
Description:
1. Player starts in middle of the work area with his chest on the floor, then gets up and performs action as directed by his partner (see examples in figure 1.8) who is responsible for timing the drill.
2. The player performs the activity and returns to the start; goes down to the floor and straight in to the next action as directed.
3. Player works for 30 seconds, repeating this process.
4. Player swaps role while partner works.
5. Roles keep rotating until each player has performed the exercise 3 times.

Figure 1.8 Fitness 4s

A	B	C	D
tackle bags – 'hit, pick up and roll out'	wrestle – 'groundwork'	beat the shield – 'footwork'	'shield clear'

start

Reps: Each player performs 3 reps with 60 seconds recovery between efforts. (This will be while the partner is working and the change-over time.)

Sets: 1–3 with 2 minutes rest between sets.

Variations: Use different rugby skills as required.

Tackle, hit, wrestle and run (THWR) × 2

Description:

1. Player starts with chest on floor; gets up and tackles the bag.
2. Gets up immediately after tackle (this is to encourage players to get to their feet straight after a tackle).
3. Moves forward to the next cone 5 m away, drives the hit shield and immediately drops down to the ground.
4. The player holding the hit shield picks up a ball, drops the shield and the two players wrestle for 5 seconds for the ball.
5. The working player then sprints around a cone 10 m away and back to the shield man; goes down to chest and up; drives shield, goes down and up and wrestles for the ball for 5 seconds.
6. Then makes the tackle and sprints back to start position.
7. Players swap roles.

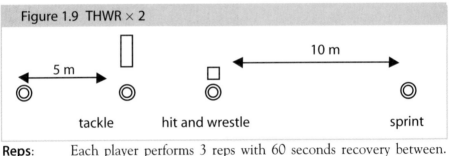

Figure 1.9 THWR × 2

10 m

5 m

tackle   hit and wrestle   sprint

Reps: Each player performs 3 reps with 60 seconds recovery between. (This will be while the partner is working and the change-over time.)

Sets: 1–3 sets with 2 minutes between sets.

Variations: Use different rugby-specific movements.

Conditioning with games

Playing games such as Aussie Rules is an excellent way of breaking up training and making a fun yet competitive activity for the players. Games can be used as a tool for the coach to develop fitness, game sense, skills and decision making.

Touch is the most commonly played game in rugby sessions, although it is quite often poorly organised and can have more negative than positive effects. Games need to be strictly refereed and monitored to be effective. Following are some examples of how touch can be used for conditionin.

Touch, run and tackle, or shield clear

Touch with small numbers will result in a quick-tempo game and the anaerobic systems being worked to a large degree, as there will be few breaks and a lot of sprinting and quick running. As a result the aerobic system will be recruited to provide energy and be worked hard to promote recovery. Putting a hitting drill in makes the game more specific to the demands of a real game without the physical contact.

Description:

Select 2 teams of no more than 8-a-side (mix of positions depending on aims).

1. Play across half a pitch with the touchlines as the try lines.
2. Lay down a set number of touches or time for possession.
3. After each touch player goes to ground (or first player rips the ball and passes if he stays on his feet).
4. Defending team have to be kept 3 m back from ruck/maul area.
5. All attackers have to be within red zone (coned line 15 m from try line) when the team scores.
6. Conceding team sprint to tackle bags on halfway line and make 4 tackles (down/up, hit). Attackers hold bags for them.
7. Once complete, both teams resume playing.

The length of time that you play will affect the way the energy systems are stressed. Playing for a greater length of time will require more aerobic input; short games with a recovery period in between will result in a higher intensity and more anaerobic effort.

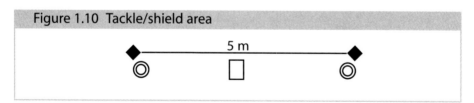

Figure 1.10 Tackle/shield area

5 m

Stress technique and getting up quickly after going to ground at the cones.

Reps: 4 × 4-minute games with 1 minute recovery between
or
2 × 10-minute games with 2 minutes recovery between.

Variations: Replace tackles with shield clears.
Teams, on scoring or conceding, have to send 2 players around cones of varying distance away from the pitch (5–20 m) which relate to their team. This will require them to communicate while

tired and will produce broken defensive and attacking lines. As soon as any player is back on the pitch, play resumes.

2-ball touch

Using 2 balls conditions the game more and means players have to begin to think of the best tactics to employ to utilise the second ball. The second ball means that when a player is touched he immediately has to perform a follow-up move in order to get the next ball in play; this increases the stress on the anaerobic and aerobic systems to provide energy.

1. Apply the same rules and pitch dimensions as the previous drill.
2. After being touched, a player places the ball on the ground and sprints to play the second ball. Only the person who has been touched can play the second ball.

Reps: 4×4-minute games with 1 minute recovery between
or
2×10-minute games with 2 minutes recovery between.

Variations: Use variations as described above.

Developing the rugby athlete

Long-term athlete development (LTAD)

Many players make it to the top in spite of an unstructured training programme rather than because of a well-designed plan. The RFU has recognised the fact that it takes between 8 and 12 years of training to produce an elite performer, and has devised a strategy to maximise the potential of young players through the work of Istvan Bayli.

This LTAD strategy is based on the required technical, tactical, mental and physiological requirements of playing rugby at the highest level. Through his research Bayli has recognised that there are key times in individuals' maturation (windows of opportunity) when certain physical components need to be brought on in order to maximise gains and to achieve the best from players' genetic make-up.

Trainability

This refers to the genetic endowment of athletes, as they respond individually to specific stimuli and adapt to it accordingly. However, there are 'critical' or 'sensitive' periods of accelerated adaptation or improvement of endurance, strength, speed and skill, which are often not considered during planning. It is during these critical periods that children and adolescents are physiologically most receptive to acquiring skills and/or improving specific physical attributes such as strength, endurance and so on.

The critical periods for the accelerated improvement of speed and power occur for boys between the ages of 7 and 9, and 13 and 16; for girls, these occur between the ages of 6 and 8, and 11 and 13.

Bayli's LTAD strategy has had rugby content added to it – for instance, the stage at which certain types of tackles or an understanding of a particular defensive strategy should be introduced. With coaches using this framework, the development of players will be structured and tailored to individual needs based on scientific principles.

The aim of this strategy is to produce elite players at the top end of the game, although it does also underpin the very ethos of coaching at all levels – to provide the opportunity for each player to reach his/her full potential. It is also crucial for all coaches to be aware of and understand this approach in order for elite players to emerge and develop. It is not until the early teenage years that the academy system begins to work for these players, so the early stages of this strategy need to be implemented mainly by parents, youth club coaches and teachers.

The RFU coaching courses have been rewritten to include LTAD as an integral part of the knowledge required by rugby coaches. The RFU has produced video resources, as well as the RFU Long Term Athlete Development document. This will ensure coaches have the information required in order to improve their knowledge, and the primary aim of individual player development.

Physical literacy

One of the most important periods of motor development for children is between the ages of 9 and 12. During this time children are developmentally ready to acquire the fundamental movement skills that are the cornerstones of all athletic development.

These fundamental skills include running, throwing, jumping, hopping and bounding – the ABCs of athletics. The introduction of the ABCs of athleticism (agility, balance, co-ordination, speed) during this period will lay the foundation of athletic excellence for later years. If physiological abilities are not developed during these critical periods, the opportunity for optimum development is lost and cannot be retrieved at a later time. Accelerated improvement for endurance coincides with the onset of Peak Height Velocity (PHV), the age of maximal growth in stature; it is at this time that the aerobic system is highly trainable. Boys generally reach their PHV at 14 (+/– 1 year) and girls at 12(+/– 1 year). Monthly measurements of height will help to establish when a player reaches his/her PHV and ensure training needs are adapted accordingly. Normal monthly growth will be between 1 and 2 cm; if this increases to 2–3 cm for a month and then 3–4 cm the following month, the PHV has started.

Training will bring about improvements in athletic ability, but the critical periods should be used to induce accelerated maximum development. It must be noted that the physical ages from the Learning to Train stage onwards are general guidelines. The individual tempo of development/maturation will influence how individuals will reach the various stages of long-term development, although they all will go through the same stages. Some early-maturing young people may have as much as a four-year physiological advantage over their late-maturing peers (Wilmore and Costill, 1994). It is therefore strongly recommended that those developing early should have their growth patterns monitored and taken into consideration.

Rugby fitness and LTAD

FUNdamental (6–8 years) and learning to train (9–11 years)

Basic health-related exercise should be encouraged with children playing a variety of games, sports and activities that encourage them to be active. No specific conditioning needs to be followed, just regular and varied physical exercise.

Training to train (12–14 years)

Depending on their stage of physical development, children of this age can cope with greater amounts of anaerobic exercise, though this should be limited. The aerobic system is developing and when they experience their growth spurt, their potential to maximise aerobic capacity is greatest.

Training to compete (15–17 years), learning to win and training to win (18 years+)

The full range of energy system training should be incorporated into a player's training programme. Intensity and volume need to be carefully monitored along with playing commitments to allow maximum development.

Chronological age is not the best way of predicting a child's readiness for a type of training and this needs to be accounted for when developing any training programme. With this in mind, from 16 years of age the energy systems are generally ready for full sport-specific training.

Summary

The time that most coaches have available specifically for conditioning is 20–30 minutes in the first of two weekly sessions. As such, it is important to carry out training that best reflects the demands of the sport within this time. The pre-season is critical for developing a base level of fitness and then making it more rugby-specific as the season approaches. In-season time needs to be allocated to work on this in club sessions, as well as players carrying out their own training.

CHAPTER 2

The training year

As coaches the contact time we have with players is often restricted to two short training sessions in the week or a couple of hours on a Sunday morning. In order to make the most of these sessions it is important to plan the activity that will take place. As a coach you should ask yourself the following question when planning a session: 'Does this session represent one part of a greater picture, or is it an individual session that has no bearing on the long-term athletic and technical needs of the team and individual?' If the answer is the latter then you are not managing your contact time effectively and need to consider devising an overall plan for the season's training – the periodised year.

This chapter is designed to familiarise you with the basic principles of planning training programmes for teams or individuals, in order to ensure that they maximise their potential.

Macrocycle – the whole training period, generally a year or season.

Mesocycle – the macrocycle is divided into shorter mesocycles in which specific fitness aims are targeted.

Microcycle – individual training sessions that work towards the aim of the mesocycle.

Breaking the year up into stages (mesocycles) allows for specific goals to be set for the training that will take place within that period. For physical components of fitness these can be tested at the beginning and end of the stage to assess the gains that have been made and the success of the particular cycle. By periodising the year you will be able to implement a structured and co-ordinated training programme – long- and short-term targets related to this will help to provide the structure to achieve the final goal.

A major function of the periodised year is to strike a balance between intensity, frequency and volume of work. If not enough time is allowed for recovery between sessions then there will be little opportunity for physical adaptation to take place. A lack of recovery time results in players training while in a fatigued state, which negates the effectiveness of training. Whereas fitness has a positive effect on performance, fatigue produces the opposite, so by not tapering the amount of physical conditioning prior to competition you are increasing the likelihood of poor performance. This was a major criticism of the Lions' training methods in Australia in 2001, when a number of the players felt they overtrained in the later stages of the tour. Tapering should take place in the lead-up to matches, competitions and throughout the training year.

Adaptation and the overcompensation cycle

Physical improvement (adaptation) is dependent on appropriate work volume/intensity and sufficient regeneration/recovery time (overcompensation).

Training in stage B (see figure 2.1) will have a negative effect on performance and will not bring about physical adaptation/improvement due to insufficient recovery time. Training should take place in stage C as overcompensation has occurred and training will be most beneficial as a result. Training in stage D means that the benefits in training are not as great as in stage C as the body has returned to its normal state.

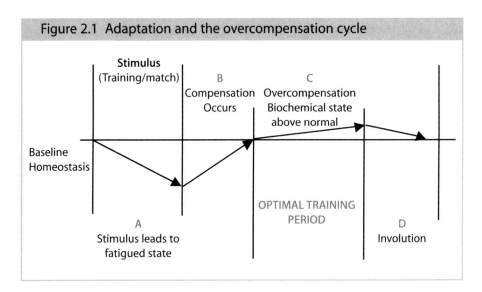

Figure 2.1 Adaptation and the overcompensation cycle

Intensity of training determines the time required to recover to state of over-compensation:

- Aerobic/low-intensity recovery can take place within 6 hours.
- Anaerobic/high-intensity recovery can take over 24 hours depending on demands made on the central nervous system.

(Yakovlev, 1967)

Single, double or multiple periodisation

Depending on age, standard and competitive cycles, your year's plan could comprise single, double or multiple periodisation. This refers to the number of competitive cycles during the training period.

Multiple periodisation is generally only appropriate to elite athletes – because of their highly trained state (after 8–12 years of training), they do not need the general conditioning and preparation phase to the same extent. The high intensity and frequency of competition ensure that these athletes maintain an optimum level of fitness throughout the year. Carefully programmed boosting and break periods within their periodised year allow for physical development and prevent burnout. Table 2.1 sets out a sample single periodised year.

Table 2.1 The single periodised year

	APR	MAY	JUN	JUL	AUG
TESTING			Pre-season testing		End of pre-season testing
PHASE	Off-season		Early pre-season	Pre-season	Late pre-season
CYCLE	Transition		Preparation		
TRAINING AIMS	Active rest and strength		Strength	Strength, power and game conditioning	Power, speed and game con-ditioning

	SEPT	OCT	NOV	DEC	JAN	FEB	MAR
TESTING					Optional testing		End of season testing
PHASE	Early competition			Mid competition		Late competition	
CYCLE	Competition						
TRAINING AIMS	Develop and maintain gains made						

Adapted from Brewer, 2002 and the RFU *Technical Journal*, summer 2002, pp. 23–7.

Stages of the periodised year

There are three basic stages that make up the periodised year:

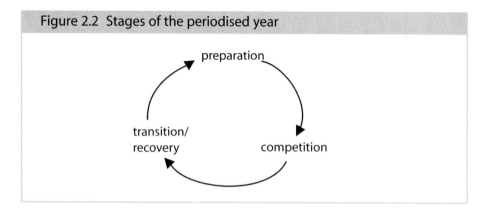

Figure 2.2 Stages of the periodised year

preparation

transition/
recovery

competition

Stage 1: Preparation

The preparation stage, as the name suggests, has the primary goal of ensuring that players are physically prepared for the demands of the season. This stage can last up to 12 weeks and it is common to break this into shorter mesocycles, which will each have a different focus in order to ensure the players are peaking at the beginning of the competitive phase.

Early pre-season

Players should have maintained a good basic level of fitness during the transition/recovery stage by cross-training and gym work. You may have little contact with your players during this cycle, but it is a critical phase in ensuring that strength gains are made which can be carried into the season. Rugby players have a very small window of opportunity in which to specifically target strength gains. Thus in the early stages of the pre-season players should be attempting to develop their strength base with regular weight training while maintaining a base level of aerobic fitness.

Pre-season

In this cycle you will have greater contact time with your players, as regular training sessions will have recommenced. In this cycle you are likely to incorporate fartlek, interval training and game-based conditioning in order to develop the anaerobic recovery powers of your players. The intensity of these sessions will increase through the weeks while the distances covered will lessen. With the season fast approaching, training should reflect the specific demands that will be placed on players during matches.

Late pre-season

The training sessions should now be very rugby-specific with high-intensity activity that mirrors the demands of the game taking place. Agility and speed training will take on increased importance as you attempt to develop the dynamic speed of movement required to break tackles and maintain body control. Players should be attempting to develop functional power and strength with plyometric training and power/weight training with high weights and low repetitions (six or less).

Stage 2: Competition

Once competitive matches begin, physical conditioning is often neglected as the more technical components of the game take on a perceived greater significance. Thus many of the benefits gained through a well-structured pre-season can be quickly negated. There is a need to maintain the gains which have been achieved, but also to try and improve the players' fitness levels throughout the competitive phase.

This requires careful management of training sessions to ensure that the individual, unit and team skills are allocated enough time as well as allowing for conditioning work. Within your training sessions the conditioning work should be integral as opposed to separate from the skill-development training. Interval runs and handling work can be carried out together, or as active recovery, and have added benefits in terms of time management, as well as making the players work on the skills while slightly fatigued.

Maintaining and developing strength, anaerobic capacity and speed are critical throughout the competition phase. It is also important to find the correct balance between high-intensity training and allowing sufficient time for the body to recover from the rigours of game play.

Table 2.2 A sample training week for an adult club player in competition

Sat	Sun	Mon	Tues	Wed	Thur	Fri
Game	Swimming – recovery session	Weights – strength/ power	Club training – anaerobic endurance	Weights – strength/ power	Club training – speed and team play	Rest/flexibility
High intensity	Low intensity	High intensity	High/ moderate intensity	High/ moderate intensity	Various	Rest

Stage 3: Transition/recovery

The end of the competitive season should not bring a shuddering halt to a player's training schedule. It provides the opportunity for a gradual decrease in the intensity and quantity of training, allowing the body to recover and recuperate from the exertion of the season. This is particularly important in a collision/contact sport such as rugby where the body and joints are placed under extreme pressure week after week. Players should choose the activities they undertake to cover a wide range of sports or exercise to maintain a core level of fitness, as well as providing a mental break from rugby-based training.

Summary

When planning your training year you need to be realistic and base it around the desires and circumstances of the players. Take into account work, social, school and family commitments when devising your plan to ensure you create a structure that is suitable to the individual and their ambitions. Effective planning is crucial to success, particularly when devising long-term development strategies for young players. However, it is important to be flexible, be guided and not constrained by your planning and be prepared to modify and change it if circumstances dictate.

CHAPTER 3

Fitness testing in rugby

At many clubs fitness testing consists of a bleep test at the first training session – the results are not used to plan any training and the test is merely a welcome back to training. There is most likely no reassessment, so carrying out this sort of token testing serves little purpose to player or coach.

A rather more scientific approach would be of great benefit in terms of monitoring physiological performance and structuring the training year, as well as having value as a psychological tool. This chapter will discuss the benefits of testing and offers a number of tests that you could use within your coaching.

Why test?

Some of the benefits of a deliberate testing policy within your club would be to:

- add structure to the coaching programme
- highlight individual/team strengths and weaknesses
- assess the effect and success of the training programme
- plan long- and short-term training programmes
- motivate players to train
- provide information for goal setting
- improve awareness and individual responsibility among players
- improve competition for places
- monitor player commitment
- act as an indicator to the possibility of injury
- assess when a player can return from an injury.

Testing for the sake of testing can have a detrimental effect on motivation and performance. The testing programme must be designed to complement the various training cycles throughout the year in order to make it a worthwhile process for all.

It is important that the players understand why they are being tested and how this relates to the game that they play. Telling a second row that he has a VO_2 max of 44 ml/kg/min and needs to get fitter does not help in achieving this goal. Testing should form part of a player development programme in which they are given advice and guidance on how to improve their future perform-ance. This should also be linked to a Personal Performance Profile (see Chapter 8) in which players can assess their own strengths and weaknesses and set agreed goals for improvement.

After position-specific fitness training (and testing) has taken place, test results need to be analysed and the positional requirements accounted for. Though all the tests described here form the core fitness requirements for rugby, their level of importance is not consistent from position to position. For example, as strength is more essential to a prop than a scrum half, a greater degree of importance might be placed on the prop's result in this area.

The most important aspect of the testing programme is not the test itself, but how the information generated is applied individually and collectively to improve performance.

What can you test?

Your tests need to be based around the components of physical fitness and their importance to rugby:

- aerobic capacity
- anaerobic capacity
- agility
- body composition
- core stability (trunk stability)
- flexibility
- muscular endurance
- power
- speed
- strength.

The tests

There will not be the time or the resources, nor is it necessary, to measure all of the above components of fitness. It is up to the coach to select the components and methods of testing which best suit the team's requirements, the level of rugby, age of players and the environmental, time and financial constraints.

Body composition

Skinfold measurements

In simplistic terms the human body is made up of fat and lean weight (muscle, bones and organs). Players often get hung up about trying to gain or lose weight, whereas in reality they should be trying to increase their lean weight or decrease their fat weight. The skinfold assessment provides a more appropriate target figure than total body weight for players and coaches to be working towards.

Body composition

Fat or lean weight can alter without necessarily affecting total body weight. If a player gains 2 kg in muscle weight and loses 2 kg in body fat the body composition will have been drastically altered, while the total body weight remains constant.

Although there is no exact percentage of body fat or lean weight that is required for success in rugby, there is a range which it is reasonable to assume will help to facilitate peak performance (6–24 per cent); the bands within this range will differ from position to position. Body fat measurements should be used to determine if weight loss/gain has been derived from fat or lean weight. A loss in body weight may be perceived as positive, but body measurements may indicate that the loss has been in lean weight as opposed to fat, and as a result fat percentage will have increased. This information is important in assessing the effectiveness of a conditioning or nutritional programme.

Measurements are usually carried out over four sites on the body – bicep, tricep, subscapular (back) and suprailiac (abdomen) on the same side of the body – using skinfold callipers (these cost between £15 and £150). The measurements indicate the amount of fat at each site – these can then be added together to give a total body fat score which can be converted into a percentage of body fat.

All good calliper sets will come with a conversion chart so there should be no need to carry out a complex series of calculations to determine body fat. There are also a number of websites that will carry out the calculation as well as providing an estimation of fat and lean body weight (www.brianmac.demon. co.uk/fatcent.htm).

Table 3.1 Desired body fat percentage for adult players

Gender	Too low (% body fat)	Good (% body fat)	Average (% body fat)	At risk (% body fat)
Males	Less than 5	6–14	15–24	25+
Females	Less than 10	11–18	19–31	32+

Source: Wilmore, J. (1993), 'Body Composition in Sport and Exercise: Directions for Future Research', *Medical Science and Sports Exercise Journal*, 15, pp. 21–31.

Calculating muscle loss/gain

This can be calculated when body weight and percentage body fat are known:

Weight of body fat = total body weight × percentage body fat
Lean body weight = body weight – weight of body fat

Example:
A player has body weight of 105 kg and 19 per cent body fat.

$105 \times 0.19 = 19.95$ kg of body fat
$105 - 19.95 = 85.05$ kg of lean weight

In order to improve reliability all measurements should be carried out by the same person. There are also a number of easy-to-use scales that will provide a body fat percentage as well as body weight; these work by sending an electric pulse around the body, which determines its result by the time the pulse takes to return (bioelectrical impedance). These devices are less accurate than the skinfold measure and fluctuate according to when they are used and what a person eats and drinks. Providing this is the only method used when testing, it will at least provide a comparable figure to work from.

Aerobic capacity

The Bleep and Yo-Yo (Bangsbo) running tests both provide an accurate prediction of a player's maximal oxygen uptake (VO_2 max) – basically the amount of oxygen that can be taken in and used, which determines the capacity to work for extended periods of time. These tests are easy to administer, requiring little equipment and cost, and are ideal for use with large groups in a small space, or when little specialist equipment or money is available. Other aerobic tests that could be used are a 12-minute timed run, where the total distance covered in the time is recorded, or a 3000 m time trial.

The 12-minute run and 3000 m time trial can be conducted at an athletics track or around a rugby pitch that has been marked out as shown below.

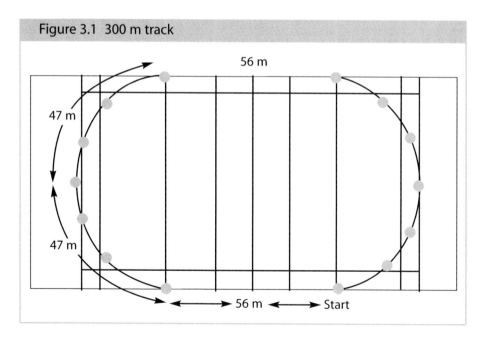

Figure 3.1 300 m track

Maximal oxygen uptake (VO$_2$ max)

This is the maximum amount of oxygen that can be taken in, transported and used by the tissues. VO$_2$ max refers to the maximum volume of oxygen consumed per minute and is the most common way of recording aerobic capacity. The most accurate way to measure this is to record the expelled air while conducting an appropriate activity. The air is then analysed to determine gas content and from this the VO$_2$ max is determined.

Table 3.2(a) Guide results for 3000 m run – amateur male players

Position	Excellent (minutes)	Good (minutes)	Average (minutes)	Poor (minutes)
Front row	<14.00	14.01–15.00	15.01–16.00	16.01+
Second row	<13.00	13.01–14.00	14.01–15.00	15.01+
Back row	<12.30	12.31–13.30	13.31–14.30	14.31+
Inside backs	<12.00	12.01–13.00	13.01–14.00	14.01+
Outside backs	<12.30	12.31–13.30	13.31–14.30	14.31+

Table 3.2(b) Guide results for 3000 m run – amateur female players

Position	Excellent (minutes)	Good (minutes)	Average (minutes)	Poor (minutes)
Front row	<16.00	16.01–17.00	17.01–18.00	18.01+
Second row	<15.00	15.01–16.00	16.01–17.00	17.01+
Back row	<14.30	14.31–15.30	15.31–16.30	16.31+
Inside backs	<14.00	14.01–15.00	15.01–16.00	16.01+
Outside backs	<14.30	14.31–15.30	15.31–16.30	16.31+

When conducting any of the above tests ensure that you have an appropriate system to record the results, and assistants to ensure that the test is being carried out correctly. The tests are maximal with players attempting to reach the highest level they can for the Bleep and Yo-Yo run, and either run as far or cover the distance as quickly as possible for the 12-minute run and 3000 m time trial respectively. Players should be heavily fatigued on completion of these tests. From experience this is not always the case as players set themselves a level to achieve, thus they determine the result rather than fatigue dictating when they finish or the time of completion.

Strength

Strength is used in many different forms in a game of rugby – it can be static, explosive or the maximum force a player can exert. These tests should be conducted in an appropriate weight training area with well-maintained equipment.

Repetition max (RM)

Any body part can be tested in this fashion, but most commonly the bench press is used as an indicator of upper body maximal strength, while the back squat or leg press can be used to do the same for the lower body.

The aim is to lift the maximum weight possible for the stated repetitions, allowing three minutes recovery between each attempt. Results should be calculated as a percentage of body weight lifted as well as overall weight lifted to give an indication of pound for pound strength.

The tests can be carried out using free weights or machines, and provide a general evaluation of dynamic muscular strength. One or three repetition max strength can be tested – for safety purposes it is advised to opt for the higher repetition tests. This is especially true when squatting, and as such the 3RM test is recommended for this assessment.

Description:

Back squat (3RM)

1. Starting weight is selected based on previous results/training and after assessment of technical proficiency.
2. Player squats so the thighs are parallel to the floor and then drives out of the squat to the standing position.
3. After a successful lift the weight is increased and repeated after an appropriate rest period of at least 3 minutes.

This test must take place in an appropriate squat rack with spotters. Many players will have been squatting for years using poor technique and partial range of motion. When testing it is important that the full range is achieved otherwise the results will be invalid due to the different ranges achieved by each player.

Bench press (1 or 3RM)

1. Starting weight is selected based on previous results/training and after assessment of technical proficiency.
2. Player lowers bar down to chest and then drives the bar up and fully extends arms.
3. After a successful lift the weight is increased and repeated after an appropriate rest period of at least 3 minutes.

An appropriate bench must be used for this test and all lifts must be spotted. Please refer to Chapter 5 where these lifts have been explored in greater detail.

Table 3.3(a) Guide results for bench and squat RM – amateur male players

		Excellent	Good	Average	Poor
Percentage of body-weight	Bench – 1RM	135	125	115	105
	Squat – 3RM	180	170	160	150

Table 3.3(b) Guide results for bench and squat RM – amateur female players

		Excellent	Good	Average	Poor
Percentage of body-weight	Bench – 1RM	115	105	95	85
	Squat – 3RM	140	130	120	110

Pulling strength

A well-balanced strength programme should consist of pushing and pulling exercises, so testing procedures should reflect this as well. The test is easy to administer and provides information that can then be used when devising strength-training programmes, as it highlights the pulling strength of players and their upper body muscular endurance.

Description:

Maximum chin-ups

1. Grip chin-up bar with palms facing towards the body.
2. Hands should be between 12 and 14 inches apart.
3. Elbows should be fully extended as player lifts him/herself up until the chin is above the bar and then returns to the start position with the elbows fully extended. This is one repetition.

4. The player continues to perform the exercise until they can no longer complete a full repetition.
5. Only full repetitions are recorded.

Table 3.4 Guide results for maximum chin-ups – amateur male players

Position	Excellent	Good	Average	Poor
Front row	8+	6	4	2
Second row	10+	8	6	4
Back row	12+	10	8	6
Inside backs	16+	14	12	10
Outside backs	16+	14	12	10

Body weight is an issue when performing this type of exercise, but athletes who can push their body weight (bench press) should be able to pull it as well. An inability to do this indicates that there is an imbalance in the pushes and pulls in the training exercises, which can also increase the risk of rotator cuff injury. To allow for a more accurate comparison of upper body push and pulling strength, 1 or 3RM chin-ups should be performed with additional weight hung from a belt; this makes the test more strength than endurance based. For example, a player who weighs 85 kg and can bench press 110 kg 1RM would need to perform a chin-up with an additional 25 kg from their belt in order to balance their pushing and pulling strength.

Power

Jump test

The dynamic and explosive nature of many of the movements in rugby – jumping for a kick-off, lifting at the line-out or pushing up from the ground – means that power is a vital component of the game. Although strength and speed are good indicators of a player's power, there are specific tests that can be used to evaluate this more accurately.

The test requires an electronic jump mat, but can be adapted if this is unavailable by using chalk or a whiteboard to mark the height jumped.

Description:
1. Players should warm up thoroughly and should include vertical jumps in their warm-up, building up to full effort jumps.
2. Player stands on the jump mat with a broomstick across his shoulders as for a back squat (if using a whiteboard, dispense with the broom and get the

43

player to reach up, keeping their heels on the floor, and make a mark where their index finger reaches).
3. Player squats down to half-squat position and explodes upwards aiming for maximal height (if using a whiteboard shade the area of board above the mark – the player extends the arm nearest the board and makes a second mark).
4. Players land in fully extended position on the mat and then flex their knees to cushion the landing.
5. The depth of the squat (counter movement) should not be controlled and should be left to the discretion of the player.
6. Player performs 3 jumps and the best score is recorded (if using a whiteboard the distance between the two marks is measured to give you a score).

Table 3.5 Guide results for counter movement jump (vertical power) – amateur players

	Excellent (cm)	Good (cm)	Average (cm)	Poor (cm)
Male	45+	35+	30+	<29
Female	35+	30+	25+	<24

Core stability (trunk stability)

Having a strong trunk is critical to rugby because of the collision-based nature of the sport – it is trunk stability that determines whether players can produce the correct and most effective position to continually take these impacts. This core/trunk strength is especially critical for good technical execution of contact and scrummaging.

Prone hold

The aim of this test is to assess the ability of the trunk to perform repeated muscular activity. The results will influence the type of power and flexibility training that is undertaken and will provide evidence as to why players may have poor body positions at the point of contact.

Description:
1. Place forearms on the ground, keeping elbows under shoulder blades.
2. Lift the legs up, keeping only the toes on the ground and hold the body up off the ground. Once in this position the assessor should begin timing.
3. Keep the head, spine and legs in a straight line and hold this position for as long as possible.

4. Concentrate on pulling the belly button towards the spine to help maintain the correct position.

5. Once the player is unable to hold this position any longer then the test is complete.

6. The assessor should monitor the form of the athlete and stop the test when form is incorrect and record the time the position was correctly held for.

7. The test can also be adapted to assess the lateral strength of the core/trunk area (transverse abdominals and obliques) by performing a side version of this exercise.

Guide results

Players should aim to hold the position for between 90 seconds and 2 minutes. Players who are unable to do so need to increase the amount of time they devote to developing core strength and stability.

Speed

Timed sprint

The ability to move the body quickly has obvious benefits in any sport – players of all positions have an advantage if they can move faster than their opponent can. Any distance can be measured but generally 30 m is used as in a game players seldom sprint further than this in one phase. Timing gates are required to produce valid and reliable results; hand timing is cheaper but produces unreliable results due to the reaction times of player and timer. Standing and/or rolling starts can be utilised in this test, which provides an accurate measure of straight-line speed. The test is simple to administer and large numbers can be tested fairly quickly.

Description:

1. Place sensors at the start line and other required distances.
2. From a standing start the player runs at full pace past the sensors.
3. From a rolling start the player starts anything from 2 to 20 m back from the start line and sprints through.
4. The best of three runs for each start type is recorded.

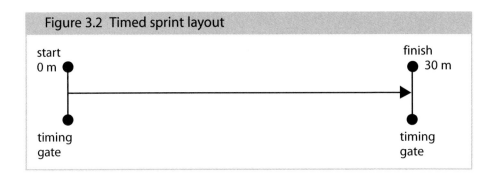

Figure 3.2 Timed sprint layout

Table 3.6(a) Guide results for 30 m sprint test (standing start) – amateur male players

Position	Excellent (seconds)	Good (seconds)	Average (seconds)	Poor (seconds)
Front row	<4.55	4.56–4.70	4.70–4.99	5.00+
Second row	<4.50	4.51–4.65	4.66–4.80	4.81+
Back row	<4.35	4.36–4.50	4.51–4.70	4.71+
Inside backs	<4.10	4.11–4.25	4.26–4.45	4.45+
Outside backs	<4.00	4.01–4.15	4.16–4.35	4.35+

Table 3.6(b) Guide results for 30 m sprint test (standing start) – amateur female players

Position	Excellent (seconds)	Good (seconds)	Average (seconds)	Poor (seconds)
Front row	<4.75	4.76–4.90	4.91–5.10	5.11+
Second row	<4.70	4.71–4.85	4.86–5.00	5.01+
Back row	<4.55	4.56–4.70	4.71–4.90	4.91+
Inside backs	<4.40	4.41–4.55	4.56–4.75	4.76+
Outside backs	<4.30	4.31–4.45	4.46–4.65	4.66+

To ensure results are reliable and valid when retesting, attempt to recreate the testing environment as accurately as possible. A track or indoor facility would be most appropriate. If a number of gates are available you could time 5 m, 10 m and 30 m splits to gauge players' acceleration as well.

Agility

Rugby is a multi-directional game and, as the competence of a player to change direction, accelerate and decelerate at pace and with control is something which is increasingly being trained, it needs to be tested. To assess this facet you could devise your own agility run to include weaving and multi-directional running. The type of agility required in rugby is also position-specific and your test should reflect this if possible. This will produce results that have more relevance and value for devising training programmes.

The tests detailed below are designed to make testing as simple as possible in a club environment while reflecting position-specific requirements. The forwards and half back test is over a shorter distance, replicating the agility required for breaking the line close to the breakdown. The centres and outside backs run is over a greater distance and the larger run-up before the change of direction mimics back line defence/attacking distances.

The start and finish positions of the test are adjacent to make hand timing more accurate – for more accurate results timing gates are required. A T-run test is often used to assess agility, but although this test is a good indicator of general ability it does not reflect the specific movement patterns found in rugby as accurately as the tests described here.

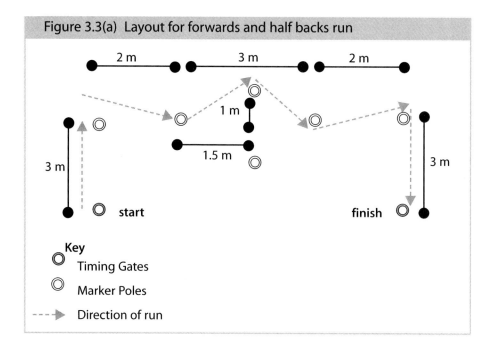

Figure 3.3(a) Layout for forwards and half backs run

2 m   3 m   2 m

1 m

1.5 m

3 m   3 m

start   finish

Key
Timing Gates
Marker Poles
Direction of run

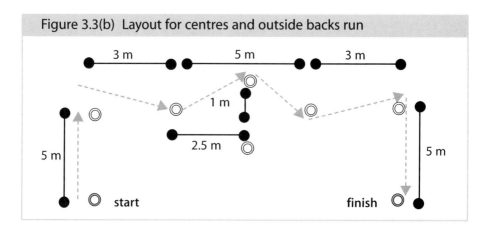

Figure 3.3(b) Layout for centres and outside backs run

Description:
1. Start behind the timing gates.
2. Sprint through the course as indicated in the diagram.
3. Ensure players sprint through the timing gates and do not decelerate before this.
4. Perform the first sprint from the left-hand side and the second from the right until you have completed two attempts in each direction.
5. The best time for runs to the left and right are recorded.
6. Allow an adequate recovery time between attempts – at least two minutes.

A non-slip surface is required to perform this test safely. As with the speed test, when re-testing try to replicate the testing conditions as accurately as possible.

Anaerobic capacity

This is arguably the most important of the tests detailed in this section as it assesses players' capacity to perform short bursts of intense activity with limited recovery periods. This replicates to a large degree the type of activity and recovery periods that occur during a game and provides a good indication of match-based fitness. The tests detailed below have again been designed to reflect to an extent the position-specific demands of the sport, with a different test for the forwards and backs.

Forwards

Description:
1. Pair off players by position, one working, the other timing and recording.
2. Record the time taken to complete each set and then add all set times together to calculate total time to complete the test.

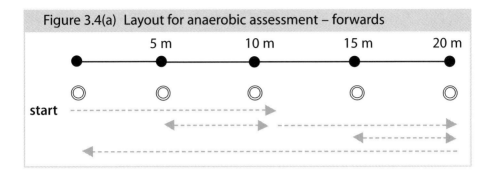

Figure 3.4(a) Layout for anaerobic assessment – forwards

3. The coach should be responsible for the running clock and informing player and timer of the rest time remaining, the content of the next set and signalling the start of the next set.
4. Player starts with chest in contact with floor and with head behind pole.
5. On start of test, player gets up and sprints out and around the pole 10 m away; runs backwards to the 5 m pole and drops down so chest is in contact with the floor.
6. Gets up and sprints out to the 10 m pole and drops down so chest is in contact with the floor.
7. Gets up, sprints forwards to the 20 m pole, then runs backwards to and around the 15 m pole.
8. Gets up, sprints out and around the 20 m pole and returns back to the start pole running forwards.

This is one repetition.

Table 3.7(a) Aide memoire and record sheet for anaerobic assessment – forwards

Running clock time (mins)	Set	Player's time
0	Start of 1 × 1 repetition	Set time:
0.45	Start of first 1 × 2 consecutive repetitions	Set time:
2.15	Start of second 1 × 2 consecutive repetitions	Set time:
4.00	Start of 1 × 4 consecutive repetitions	Set time:
6.30	Start of 1 of 1 repetition	Set time: Total time: Fatigue index:

Recovery time is decided by the time taken to complete the previous set. The start time of each set is controlled by the running clock, so the quicker a player finishes a set the longer their recovery time prior to the start of the next one.

Backs

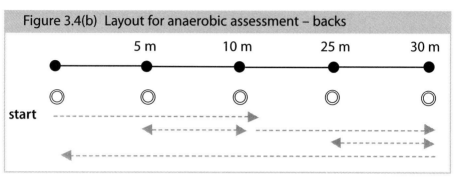

Figure 3.4(b) Layout for anaerobic assessment – backs

Description:

1. Player starts with chest in contact with floor and with head behind pole.
2. On starting the test the player gets up and sprints out and around the pole 10 m away, runs backwards to behind the 5 m pole and drops down so chest is in contact with the floor.
3. Gets up, sprints forwards to the 30 m pole, then runs backwards to and around the 25 m pole.
4. Then sprints out and around the 30 m pole and runs forwards back to the start. This is one repetition.

Table 3.7(b) Aide memoire and record sheet for anaerobic assessment – backs

Running clock time (mins)	Set	Player's time
0	Start of 1 × 1 repetition	Set time:
0.50	Start of second 1 × 1 repetition	Set time:
1.40	Start of first 1 × 2 consecutive repetitions	Set time:
3.20	Start of second 1 × 2 consecutive repetitions	Set time:
5.00	Start of third 1 × 2 consecutive repetitions	Set time:
6.30	Start of 1 of 1 repetition	Set time Total time: Fatigue index:

A fatigue index can be calculated for each athlete based on the difference between the first and last repetitions. Along with the combined time taken to perform the sets, this provides the comparative data for future assessments. A high fatigue index and combined time indicates that the player cannot maintain performance levels for repeated bouts of activity with limited rest periods. This test also highlights the last lap hero – a player whose last run is significantly quicker than their first will not have put in the desired levels of effort throughout the test.

Use different colored cones or poles to make the actions at each site easier for the player to identify with, and walk the course with the players twice before testing to ensure they understand the procedure.

Table 3.8 Guide results for anaerobic assessment – amateur male players

Position	Excellent (total time in seconds)	Good (total time in seconds)	Average (total time in seconds)	Poor (total time in seconds)
Front row	<250	251–260	261–275	276+
Second row	<240	241–250	251–265	266+
Back row	<230	231–245	246–260	261+
Inside backs	<220	221–230	231–245	246+
Outside backs	<220	221–230	231–245	246+

Planning the testing year

When to test and retest needs to be structured to complement the aims of the main training programme and the time and environmental constraints on the team. It is important not to overtest as this can have a detrimental effect on the motivation of players towards the testing procedure. Much in-season training is geared to maintaining fitness levels. As there will be little change in test results, this can have a demoralising effect on players who have trained regularly since the last test, but not registered any improvement. Testing needs to precede and follow a deliberate fitness-specific training cycle in order to assess the effectiveness of the programme.

Hiring a sports hall to carry out the tests will help to improve the reliability of your results and a different environment helps to break up the repetitive nature of club sessions. This is a particularly useful tool in the winter months when weather conditions can discourage some from attending and make it difficult to carry out any quality training outdoors.

In order to increase the reliability of the testing programme, tests should be conducted in the same order and with ample recovery time if more than one test is conducted in a session. Due to the nature of the testing, anaerobic and aerobic tests should not be carried out on the same day. Speed, power and then strength testing should precede all other assessments.

Below is a guide to the structure of the testing year – again it may not be appropriate to carry out all of the tests for the components of fitness.

1. Baseline tests

These need to be carried out at the end of the season. This will provide information regarding the condition of your players at the end of the season, as well as a reference point to compare their condition at the end of the previous season and the beginning of the new one. Whichever tests are administered here need to be reassessed in the pre-competition phase. Select from:

- aerobic
- body composition
- speed
- agility
- anaerobic endurance
- strength
- power
- core strength.

2. Pre-competition tests

Tests should be conducted prior to competition to ensure that players are making the appropriate improvements and to assess the effectiveness of the training. These also provide a little time before the beginning of competitive fixtures to fine-tune any problem areas highlighted. Tests should be the same as baseline to enable comparison:

- aerobic capacity
- body composition
- speed
- agility
- anaerobic endurance
- strength
- power
- core strength.

The strength test should be included to assess effectiveness of the building phase and to provide maintenance guide data, although if not all members of the squad are carrying out strength training, testing them is a futile exercise. The most sensible use of time is to only test those who are actively involved in a weights programme or who are about to begin one. The strength and core strength tests can be conducted away from training sessions to reduce impingement on coaching time.

It can be of benefit to conduct a further testing programme approximately six weeks after the pre-competition tests, particularly if there were major deficiencies highlighted at this stage to check if they have been rectified. However, beware of overtesting and the loss of valuable coaching time.

3. In-season tests

This testing stage should be carried out after Christmas when there may have been a decline or increase in the number of training hours. The focus at this stage is really on ensuring that sharpness and anaerobic capabilities are being maintained since the last testing phase.

It is not necessary to retest all the components from the baseline and pre-competition phase. Coaches should review the deficiencies in physical performance that have been demonstrated in games and reassess these. Individual players may require additional testing depending upon their specific training programmes and performances.

All results should be collated and kept as a reference point for future goal-setting exercises and to be compared with the baseline tests for the following season.

Testing and LTAD

While a degree of sensitivity is required when testing adults, it is of greater importance when working with children. Their emotional and social development can easily be negatively influenced by inappropriate testing and the importance placed upon the results.

FUNdamental (6–8 years), learning to train (9–11 years)

There is little to be gained from testing children at this stage due to the lack of physical growth and development that has taken place. The RFU proficiency awards should be used to introduce movement patterns and to provide tangible targets in terms of skill development in a fun and rewarding environment.

Training to train (12–14 years)

At this point there is a window of opportunity to develop aerobic capacity and speed/agility (dependent on PHV) and as such these tests become relevant. Players will be performing light resistance training and body-weight exercises, so a muscular endurance (press-ups) test as opposed to a maximum strength test could also be conducted. Again, the RFU proficiency awards are an appropriate tool to be used at this stage.

Training to compete (15–17 years), learning to win and training to win (18 years+)

Players are now reaching full physical maturation, although this occurs at different ages for each individual so training and testing need to reflect this.

Summary

Some of the tests described are fairly inexpensive – the Multi-stage Fitness Test and Yo-Yo Test cost approximately £15 and £25 respectively. Assuming that your club does not have an adequate set of weights to conduct the strength tests, these would cost something in the region of £500. Such costs can of course be offset by the fact that they should be used regularly and have a long shelf life. Much of the cost for testing could be covered by contacting a local university and arranging for their undergraduates to carry out the testing. The benefit from this is threefold: accurate testing by sports scientists; reduction in cost; and developing links with the local institute of higher education.

Whereas test results only provide an indication of the physical attributes of an individual, and provide valuable information about the strengths and weaknesses of a player, they should not be used as judgement of rugby ability. Some players loathe testing and as with exams can underperform, although in a match their contribution can vastly exceed what would be expected based on their test results.

Testing is part of the overall monitoring process – used correctly it will enable the team and individual players to bring about improvements in performance and conditioning. Remember, it is not testing that brings these gains, but how the information is applied to training.

CHAPTER 4

Speed and agility

In rugby, speed at all levels and positions is a highly prized commodity that can get players out of trouble or create chaos for the opposition. Moving quickly and with control is largely dependent on a range of factors, as set out in table 4.1 overleaf.

You often hear coaches describing players as having natural raw pace and others as not being blessed with this genetic gift. This is true in that a person's ability to run or move quickly is largely determined by the properties of their musculoskeletal system. Though you cannot create more of the muscle fibres and joint structures required to run fast, you can improve them through physical and technical training.

Table 4.1 Factors affecting speed

Factor	Explanation
Neuromuscular co-ordination	The speed and effectiveness with which nerves and muscles work together to respond to a stimulus and produce the appropriate physical response.
Muscular power	The force that is generated by the contraction or extension of the muscle.
Muscle fibre composition	The fibre composition of muscles greatly affects the speed at which the muscles work. Fast-twitch fibres contract and extend twice as fast as slow-twitch fibres and are more suited to speed and power activities.
Range of motion/flexibility	Limited flexibility reduces the force that can be generated by the muscle and hence reduces the speed and power of movements.
Technique	Poor technical execution of movement patterns results in reduced power output and wasted effort. Technical flaws prevent maximum force generation and its most effective use.

Muscle fibres

A top-class marathon runner's calf muscle (gastrocnemius) can consist of as much as 90 per cent slow-twitch fibres. This is in contrast with a sprinter, who can have as little as 25 per cent of this type of muscle fibre. These are the result of genetics and adaptations to the muscle fibres as a consequence of the specific training regimes of these different events.

It is a great advantage to be able to move a fraction of a second more quickly than an opponent in a game of rugby – an extra burst of speed can result in tries being scored or last-ditch tackles made.

Rugby speed

Speed for rugby can be broken down into three main components.

1. Acceleration speed

Commonly referred to as speed off the mark and relates to the ability to change from a stationary or slow movement to a quicker pace, for example:

- a lock sprinting from the defensive line to charge down a kick
- the scrum half breaking from the base of a scrum.

2. Maximal (top-end) speed

In a 100-metre straight-line sprint this occurs between 30 and 60 m. As players tend to be in motion before they begin sprinting in a game, it is therefore more likely that maximal speed is reached earlier in comparison to straight-line sprinting. The multi-directional nature of rugby and number of bodies on the pitch means that straight-line sprinting is rare:

- a winger reaching maximum speed while covering across the pitch to make a tackle
- centres chasing an up and under to compete in the air with the opposition full back.

Training tip – improving maximal speed and acceleration

In order to develop these qualities players will need to spend time during the pre-season devoted to speed and acceleration only. During the season, specific game-related speed and speed endurance will be the main focus of speed training. Thus the pre-season offers the player the best opportunity to develop maximal speed and acceleration.

When working with sprinters during the summer season a typical speed session might be 4 × 60 m with full recovery between each run (5 min). This allows for the full recovery of the PC system, which is critical to ensure quality of work. Speed sessions should leave you feeling refreshed, not exhausted.

3. Speed endurance

This is needed to maintain speed over longer distances (60 m+), as well as the ability to repeatedly perform short bursts of activity with small rest periods. This type of training generally involves running longer distances (100–400 m) with shorter recovery periods between repetitions and reduced rest time between sets. This type of training fits in well with training goals for the pre-season, but caution needs to be applied when prescribing this type of training to larger players due to the risk of injury from running long distances at a high intensity.

Repetitive speed

This is a rugby-specific form of speed endurance that involves performing short sprints/high-intensity bursts of activity (20–60 m) with little recovery period and little loss in speed. The multi-phase nature of rugby means that players may be called upon to work at high intensities with a short break (a few seconds) and then at a high intensity again. This is a highly specific form of speed training for the demands of the game, for example:

- the defensive line moving up and back to put pressure on attackers, staying onside and then turning to chase a kick
- props sprinting to clear a succession of rucks
- the stand-off making a break, clearing a ruck and then supporting the next ball carrier.

Table 4.2 Approximate work–rest ratios and volume for speed training

Component of speed	Work–rest ratio	Distance/session
Acceleration	1:3	300 m
Top-end speed	1:4	500 m
Speed endurance	1:1	2000 m

All of these components of speed need to be included in a rugby player's speed training programme.

Training methods

In order to get quick you need to train quick – speed training is therefore performed with near maximal effort, low volume and with long recovery times between repetitions and sets. Speed training should be complemented by weight training, plyometrics and technique (running mechanics) training to bring about maximal benefit. Sprint training should take place on an appropriate surface, such as a synthetic track or good-quality grassed area. Performing speed training on a muddy pitch is counterproductive.

There is a tendency for most speed training to take place from a standing start because it has transferred from athletics. In rugby, however, players are normally in motion to some extent when they begin sprinting, thus the training should replicate this.

Sprint start positions
- walking
- 3-point start
- rolling starts (jogging or quicker as desired)
- change of direction into the sprint
- jumping
- turning (90 degrees, 180 degrees etc.)
- from the ground (face down, sitting, on back etc.)
- backwards running to forwards sprint (off- to on-side).

All speed and agility work should take place immediately following the warm-up when the body is appropriately prepared. This means that gains will be maximised as players have not been fatigued by other training activity.

Acceleration speed training

Hill sprints 15–40 m (slight incline)
Uphill sprints force the calf muscles to work harder; this increases calf strength and results in less contact time and increased stride length when running on the flat.

Rugby relevance – improved acceleration from the different start positions that occur during a game.

Set 1:	8 × 15 m
Set 2:	5 × 30 m
Set 3:	3 × 40 m

Intensity:	90–100 per cent.
Repetitions:	As detailed above.
Sets:	As detailed above.
Recovery:	Walk back recovery between repetitions (runs) plus 30 seconds and 2 minutes rest between sets.
Progressions:	Multi-directional running can be included. Use different start positions.

Sprint pyramid (10–30 m)

Rugby relevance – improved acceleration from different start positions that occur during a game.

Set 1:	6 × 10 m
Set 2:	4 × 20 m
Set 3:	2 × 30 m
Set 4:	4 × 20 m
Set 5:	6 × 10 m

Intensity:	90–100 per cent.
Repetitions:	As detailed above.
Sets:	As detailed above.
Recovery:	Walk back recovery between repetitions (runs) plus 30 seconds and 2 minutes rest between sets.
Progressions:	Multi-directional running can be included. Use different start positions.

Mechanics of acceleration, sprinting and deceleration

The need to change direction to avoid contact, make a tackle or react to a bouncing ball requires the ability to accelerate and decelerate quickly with control and is a skill that players should spend time developing. If improvements are to be made in this area, the techniques involved in these actions need to be practised and then applied in rugby-specific situations. Many players have never been shown how the body and limbs should co-ordinate in order to accelerate and decelerate. Overleaf is a summary of the key principles of accelerating and decelerating that can be taught as a discipline in its own right or combined with any skill-based drill. The example uses a three-point stance as the start position, but the principles transfer into any situation when a player is trying to pick up or reduce speed.

Three-point stance

The three-point stance is a good position from which to accelerate, and in defensive situations players often adopt this as it provides an excellent base to generate the force to move quickly towards the attackers.

Key principles:

- Body weight is spread evenly over the three limbs that are in contact with the ground.
- When possible the dominant leg should be the furthest back.
- Only the balls of both feet are on the ground about hip width apart. The front leg should be bent to about 90 degrees and the rear leg to 100–130 degrees.
- Toes for rear foot should be 6–12 inches behind the heel of the front foot (depending on size and comfort of position for the player).
- If the left foot is furthest back the fingers of the left hand should be on the floor. This will encourage correct arm and leg co-ordination when the player drives off.
- Activate the core by pulling the belly button towards the spine to keep the back in a neutral position.

Acceleration

Key principles:

- Player drives from the ball of the rear foot to create initial drive.
- As the rear leg swings through, the front leg extends and pushes against the ground to provide additional force for driving off.
- As the rear leg swings through, the corresponding arm will drive back and the opposite arm will come forward (contralateral arm movement).

- Elbows should be flexed at 90 degrees and the arms should drive back powerfully from the shoulders so that the elbow goes up to or beyond the level of the shoulders.
- Body should be tilting forward and the head relaxed with the player looking up through the eyebrows rather than holding the head high.

Drive

Key principles

- For the first few strides the emphasis should be on powerful arm drives and pushing off from the ground to generate force.
- A rapid stride rate (frequency) should be encouraged with short powerful steps and limited ground contact time, driving forwards not upwards.
- Towards the end of this phase arm drive is reduced – hands move from 'hips to lips'.
- Forward lean reduces as player approaches the end of this phase.

As rugby is a contact sport acceleration should be practised with this in mind. Players should practise accelerating having been knocked off balance or having hit a contact shield to replicate accelerating after the contact situations that arise in rugby.

Maximal speed

Key principles:

- Knee lift increases and becomes faster – as a result stride length increases.
- Player rises up to full height.
- As the leg pushes off the ground, it should fold up towards the hip and buttocks.
- Shoulders and jaw should be relaxed ('jelly jaw').

Braking/deceleration

Key principles:

- Reduce stride length and increase strike rate with the floor.
- Use rapid contralateral arm drives to assist braking; as braking occurs arms will work more in front of the body than behind in order to slow you down.

- Lowering the centre of gravity by sitting down through the hips with the core muscles activated will also help to slow down the speed that you are moving at.

Players should practise decelerating at progressively quicker speeds to develop this skill until they can decelerate from full speed. Once players are competent at decelerating in a straight line, multi-directional running and braking should be developed.

Table 4.3 Target stopping times from different speeds

Speed	Steps to stop
50 per cent	3 steps
75 per cent	5 steps
100 per cent	7 steps

(Source: Plisk, Steven (2000), *Essentials of Strength Training and Conditioning*, Human Kinetics, Champaign, Ill.)

Agility is heavily dependent on the ability to decelerate and change direction quickly, so this should receive as much attention in training programmes as acceleration.

Improving sprinting mechanics

Correct running mechanics can greatly aid a player's potential to move at speed. This is of most benefit at a young age, as learning the correct techniques early can prevent bad habits developing. Technical improvements in running style will be of most benefit to those who are not naturally quick as the efficiency of movement will be significantly improved. England Conditioning

Coach, Calvin Morris, believes that those who are naturally quick will possibly derive greater speed improvement from power/strength training as opposed to technical speed work. With the limited contact times coaches have with players, correct running technique should be reinforced as part of general session work and highlighted during warm-up activity.

Stride length and frequency

Speed production is the result of the length and frequency of your stride. Improving the efficiency of both of these will bring about gains in speed. The greater the force that can be applied against the ground, the greater the stride length; and the more frequently this can occur without limiting stride length, the quicker the player will move. Speed training should look to improve leg power for greater force, and leg speed for increased strike frequency.

Here are some simple drills that can be practised to develop the technical aspects of sprinting or included in the latter part of a warm-up.

Sprint technique drills

Technique drills should be performed at speed once the action has been learned in order to bring about the greatest gains.

Arm drive (improves arm movement)

- Drive the elbows back from the shoulders to hit the palms of partner's hand to encourage correct range of motion.
- Relax the shoulders and keep the elbows bent at 90 degrees.
- Range of movement should be from hips to lips with arms moving straight ahead, not across the body.
- Perform two sets of 10 drives.

Weighted arm drives can be performed by holding a light dumbbell in each arm to improve the power of movement. A contrast set can be performed after this to increase gains.

Butt flick (improves leg speed)

- To develop the speed the leg 'folds up' and is returned to the ground.
- While jogging the heel is flicked back towards the buttocks – do not force the leg up, but push off the floor and let it swing up.
- Perform two sets of 10 flicks.

Perform as a single-leg exercise and/or through hurdles.

High knees (improves knee drive and reduces ground contact time)

- Leaning slightly forward, start with the knee up just above hip height with the toes pointing down.
- Encourage player to return ball of foot to ground quickly and rebound up rapidly with minimal ground contact.
- Perform two sets of 10 high knees.

Perform as a single-leg exercise and/or through hurdles.

Fast feet (increases strike rate and reduces ground contact time)

- From jogging take as many steps as possible over a distance of 10 m.
- Knees are kept low and there should be no heel contact with the floor; body leans slightly forward.
- Encourage arm movement and feet placement to be in front, not behind body.
- Jog for 10 m and repeat.
- Perform two sets of fast feet.

Perform sideways and backwards, and use ladder drills to develop this.

Maximal speed training

Maximal runs (30–60 m)

Use rolling starts to better reflect the demands and situations that occur during matches and to decrease the time taken to reach top speed.

Rugby relevance – improved acceleration from different start positions that occur during a game.

Set 1:   5 × 40 m
Set 2:   3 × 60 m
Intensity: 90–100 per cent.
Repetitions: As detailed above.
Sets: As detailed above.
Recovery: Walk back recovery between repetitions (runs) plus 3 min, and 4 min rest between sets.

Progressions:
- Multi-directional running can be included.
- Use different start positions.

Resistance runs (30–60 m)

Perform the runs with the added resistance of a parachute or dragging a sled. At the end of each set perform one run without the resistance (contrast*).

Rugby relevance – improved acceleration and maximal speed from different start positions that occur during a game.

Set 1:   3 × 30 m (plus 1 × contrast).
Set 2:   3 × 40 m (plus 1 × contrast).
Set 3:   3 × 50 m (plus 1 × contrast).

Intensity: 90–100 per cent.
Repetitions: As detailed above.
Sets: As detailed above.
Recovery: Walk back recovery between repetitions (runs) plus 3 minutes, and 4 minutes rest between sets.

Progressions:
- Multi-directional running can be included with the parachute.
- Two parachutes can be used to increase resistance.
- Use different start positions.

* Contrast training is described in more detail later in this chapter on page 70.

Speed endurance training

30-second target U-runs

Players aim to run as far as they can in 30 seconds. Place cones at 10 m internals between the try lines for the length of the pitch – this will provide the measurements for the players to use as targets. When players reach the far try line they turn around and run back.

Set 1: 6 × 30-second runs (set target distance for positions to achieve in runs).

30 seconds recovery between runs and 2 minutes rest between sets.

Set 2: 4 × 30-second runs.

30 seconds recovery between runs and 1½ minutes between sets.

Set 3: 2 × 30-second runs.

Table 4.4 Approximate distances for adult players with good to high fitness levels

Positions	Distance (m)
Props and second rows	120+
Back row and hooker	140+
Centres and half backs	160+
Full back and wings	180+

Intensity: 70–90 per cent.
Repetitions: As detailed above.
Sets: As detailed above.
Recovery: As detailed above.

Progressions:
• Multi-directional running can be included.
• Use different start positions.

Repetitive speed drills

20–40 m repeat speed recovery.

Set 1: 6 × 20 m sprint, 10 seconds recovery between repetitions (runs). 1½ minutes rest between sets.

Set 2: 4 × 40 m sprint, 30 seconds recovery between repetitions (runs). 2 minutes rest between sets.

Set 3: 6 × 30 m sprint, 20 seconds recovery between repetitions (runs).

Intensity: 80–90 per cent.
Repetitions: As detailed above.
Sets: As detailed above.
Recovery: As detailed above.

Progressions:
• Multi-directional running can be included.
• Use different start positions.
• Use resistance equipment.

Cross run repeat speed recovery

1. Player sprints forward to line 5 m away and then runs backwards to return to start position.
2. Performs this pattern twice and on third forward run sprints a further 10 m to a cone nominated by the coach (this is one repetition).
3. Player walks back to the start position and repeats the pattern.

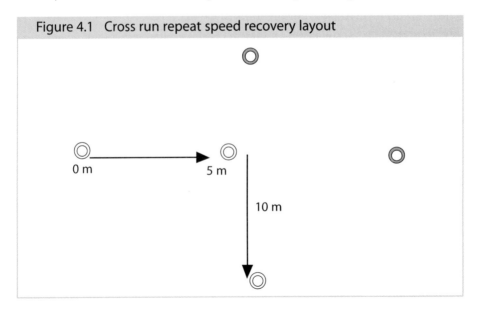

Figure 4.1 Cross run repeat speed recovery layout

0 m

5 m

10 m

Intensity: 80–90 per cent.
Repetitions: 3
Sets: 3–6
Recovery: Walk back recovery between repetitions and one minute rest between sets.

Progressions:
- Multi-directional running can be included.
- Use different start positions.
- Contact and ball skills can be included in the activity to make it more rugby-specific.

Change of pace

Rugby requires players to vary the speed they are running at and this 'change of pace' needs to be practised. Hollow sprints are an excellent way of training this aspect of rugby-specific speed. Hollows involve sprinting for a set distance, slowing down and then accelerating again for a set distance. Hollows can be designed for any of the three components of speed for rugby by altering the distances of the sprint and ease-off sections. An example of a hollow sprint drill for acceleration is detailed below.

Hollow 15–10–5

Rugby relevance – change of pace, acceleration and deceleration (distances should be altered to tailor to positional needs).

1. Player sprints for 15 m then eases off.
2. Then accelerates away at the next cone for 10 m and decelerates at the following cone.
3. Accelerates at the next cone for 5 m.

Intensity: 100 per cent
Repetitions: 6
Sets: 3
Recovery: Walk back recovery between runs plus 15 seconds, and 3 minutes rest between sets.

Progressions:
- Multi-directional running can be included.
- Use resistance and assistance equipment.
- Use different start positions.

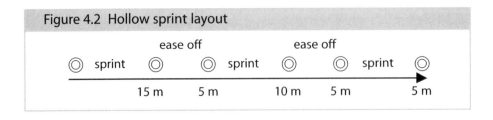

Figure 4.2 Hollow sprint layout

Speed training equipment

There are a variety of products now available to the coach and player to assist the development of speed, such as parachutes, sleds and resistance and over-speed belts. These devices help to add variety to training and can be made rugby-specific as well as allowing greater gains to be made through resisted or assisted work.

Anyone using such products should attend an appropriate training course to ensure they are fully aware of the safety aspects and benefits of such resources. Details of courses and equipment can be found at www.saqinternational.com.

Assisted running (overspeed training)

This trains the fast-firing nerve cells that co-ordinate and control leg-muscle activity, and teaches muscle cells to function at accelerated speeds. This is possible as body weight is supported/reduced so the muscles are carrying less weight than they normally have to cope with. This helps to increase leg speed, and muscle memory ensures that this quicker firing rate is remembered, learned and transferred when running unassisted.

Resistance runs (functional overload)

Performing game-relevant activity with increased loads/resistance causes muscles to work harder and adaptation/improvement to take place. Hill sprints, parachutes, sled drags and bungee cord work are examples of this type of training.

Contrast runs

When working with assistance or resistance equipment you should always perform a repetition (run) without the assistance/resistance to enable the muscle memory transfer to take place.

Overspeed training

Rest and recovery times need to be manipulated depending upon the type of speed you are trying to develop. For maximal speed and acceleration, rest and recovery needs to be high; for repetitive rugby speed endurance the times will be lower. The drill below is based on repetitive speed for rugby.

Straight line overspeed

1. Two players are linked by a bungee belt 6 m apart so the belt is taut.
2. Player A sprints out and past B, and decelerates at the next cone.

Intensity: 100 per cent.
Repetitions: 5 plus 1 contrast run.
Sets: 3
Recovery: Walk back recovery plus 30 seconds between repetitions (runs) and 2 minutes rest between sets (rest while partner works).

Figure 4.3 Straight line overspeed layout

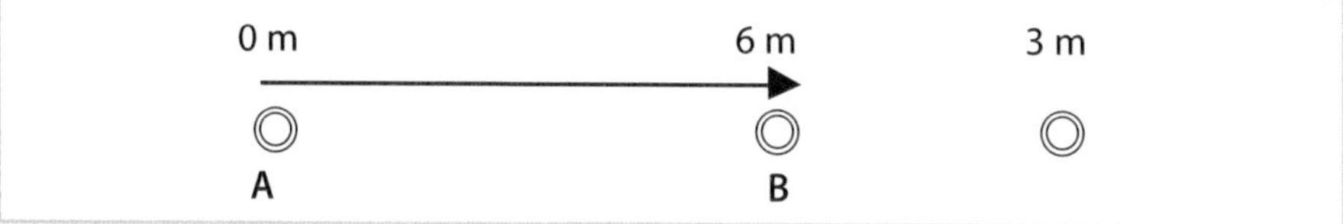

0 m   6 m   3 m

A   B

Progressions:
* Receive and give a pass on the run.
* Add a change of direction into the run.

A number of the drills in the agility section on pages 73–81 can also be performed with overspeed.

Resistance training

Resisted shield drive

Rugby relevance – acceleration.

1. Two players are linked by a bungee belt.
2. The working player sprints out 3 m and drives the shield being held by another player back 1 m, then sprints backwards to the start position.

Figure 4.4: Resisted shield drive layout

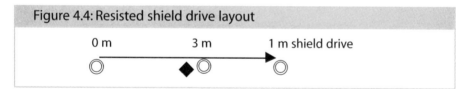

0 m   3 m   1 m shield drive

Intensity: 100 per cent.
Repetitions: 6 plus 1 contrast run.
Sets: 3
Recovery: 2 minutes rest between sets (rest while partner works).

Resisted X-run

Rugby relevance – acceleration and repetitive speed.

1. Two players are linked by a bungee belt (the second player needs to move forward and mirror the movements of the working player to maintain the resistance through the course).
2. The working player sprints out 3 m and drives the shield being held by another player back 1 metre.
3. The player then sprints backwards to the next cone, sprints forwards and around the cone and runs backwards to the start position.
4. Players repeat this course for the set number of repetitions

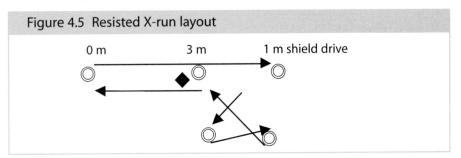

Figure 4.5 Resisted X-run layout

Intensity: 100 per cent.
Repetitions: 6 plus 1 contrast run.
Sets: 3
Recovery: 2 minutes rest between sets (rest while partner works).

Progressions:
- Receive and give a pass on the run.
- Use the different start positions described on page 59.

30 m parachute swerve

Rugby relevance – maximal speed, balance and change of direction at pace (distances should be altered for positional needs and to work different components of speed).

1. Player is wearing a parachute for added resistance.
2. From a 5 m rolling start the player accelerates and sprints through the course, following the cones.

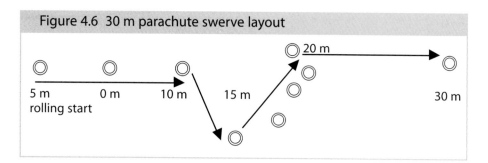

Figure 4.6 30 m parachute swerve layout

Intensity: 100 per cent.
Repetitions: 5 repetitions and 1 contrast run.
Sets: 2 or 3.
Recovery: Walk back recovery between runs plus 45 seconds, and 3 minutes rest between sets.

Progressions:
• Multi-directional running can be included.
• Use resistance and assistance equipment.
• Use different start positions.

Apart from the physiological benefits that the increased firing of muscle cells has on speed, there are also psychological gains from this type of training. The assisted and contrast runs will allow the player to feel a significant increase in the speed they are moving at. This can result in an increased level of confidence – for players whose game is based on speed, the need to 'feel' quick is linked to their physical performance, and this training provides an opportunity to reinforce positive self-image.

Agility

Although straight-line speed is important in rugby, the ability to move at pace and brake at pace, with control and change of direction, is of greater value. The prop forward spinning out of the contact area and the winger feigning to go on the inside and then taking his man on the outside are examples of how this is applied in rugby. Improvements in agility can be brought about through training and should be included in each player's training programme. All players should work on their agility from stationary and rolling starts over short (1–5 m) and longer (20–30 m) distances.

The distances covered and changes in direction while sprinting differ between positions. As such there is a need for some specialisation in agility work to reflect the position-specific requirements. For example, scrum halves need to be able to dart away from the base of scrums and rucks, while full backs and wings often have space to run at defenders and need to develop their ability to change direction over longer distances while at full speed. However, all players should have a basic level of competence, as props will find themselves in open field and wingers and full backs will sometimes be attacking close to rucks and mauls.

Changing direction at pace requires whole body control, and someone who has good straight-line speed can be markedly slower when required to change direction. Core and rotational training should also be carried out to help bring about the greatest development of this skill.

Ladder drills have made a significant difference to a player's footwork – being able to control foot placement, co-ordination and stride frequency underpins the ability to change direction. Ben Cohen is one England player who has greatly increased his effectiveness at international level as a result of improvements in this area. Ladders also play an important role in improving the core balance, co-ordination and control of players and should be used to reinforce this whenever possible.

It is equally important, however, to analyse the movements that commonly take place on the rugby field. From this coaches should introduce practices that have position relevance, rather than just putting players through a series of ladder-based footwork exercises.

Rugby-specific movements

The ladder-based footwork drills below are taken from SAQ Rugby (A & C Black, 2001) which provides an excellent reference point from which to develop your own rugby-specific practices.

Fast Foot Ladder – single run

Aim: To develop fast feet with control, precision and power.

Description: The player covers the length of the ladder by placing one foot in each ladder space. Return to the start by jogging back on the outside of the ladder.

Key teaching points:
- Maintain correct running form/mechanics.
- Start slowly and gradually increase the speed.
- Maintain an upright posture.
- Stress that quality not quantity is important.

Sets and reps: 3 sets of 4 reps with 1 minute recovery between each set.

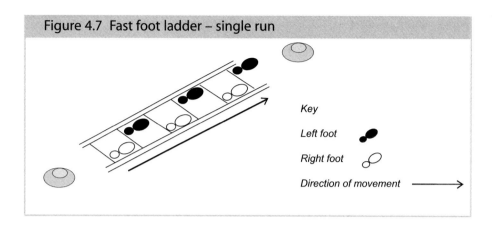

Figure 4.7 Fast foot ladder – single run

Key

Left foot

Right foot

Direction of movement

Fast Foot Ladder – up, across and backwards

Aim: To develop speed and control of acceleration when pressing/attacking the opposition. To develop controlled lateral pressing skills and co-ordinated backward movement prior to turning and chasing.

Description:

Place two ladders in a 'T' formation with one cone at the end of each ladder. The player accelerates down the ladder using single steps. On reaching the ladder crossing the end, the player moves laterally either left or right using short lateral steps. On coming out of the ladder the player then moves backwards in a side-on running motion, keeping both the eyes and head looking forwards.

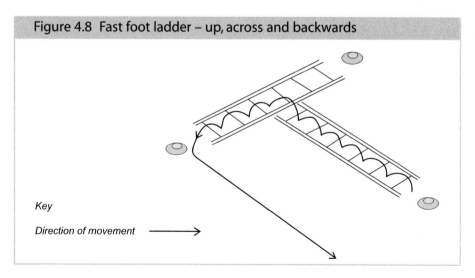

Figure 4.8 Fast foot ladder – up, across and backwards

Key

Direction of movement

Key teaching points:
- Maintain correct running form/mechanics.
- Use a strong arm drive when transferring from linear to lateral steps.
- When moving backwards keep the head and eyes up.
- Do not skip backwards.

Sets and reps: 3 sets of 4 reps with 1 minute recovery between each set (2 moving to the left and 2 moving to the right).

Fast Foot Ladder – with a ball

Aim: To develop fast feet, speed and agility while incorporating game-specific ball control.

Description:
Place a Fast Foot ladder with a cone at each end approx 1 m away. While a player is performing Fast Foot drills down the ladder either laterally or linearly, a second player standing 2 m away from the ladder in a central position feeds the ball in to the player at different heights, requiring the first player to catch, control and return the ball.

Key teaching points:
- Concentrate on good footwork patterns.
- Ensure that correct technical skills are used when controlling and returning the ball.
- Ensure that the player performing the drill returns to correct running form/ mechanics after returning the ball.

Sets and reps: 3 sets of 6 reps with 1 minute recovery between each set.

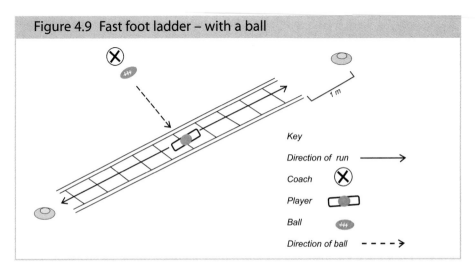

Figure 4.9 Fast foot ladder – with a ball

Fast Foot Ladder – with passing

Aim: To develop fast feet and agility while incorporating rugby-specific ball control and passing combination drills.

Description:

Place a ladder in an upside-down 'L' pattern with an identically shaped ladder next to the first approx 2 m away. Place cones at the start and end of each ladder (1 m away). Place another two cones 15 m away and 1 m apart in line with the centre space. At the end of one ladder, place a ball. Both players start with linear Fast Foot drills then transfer to lateral drills as the ladder dictates. Player 1 accelerates on to the ball supplied by the coach. Player 1 passes the ball across the grid to player 2, who on receiving the ball cuts inside and performs a switch movement with player 1, who receives the ball and straightens up.

Key teaching points:
- Maintain correct running form/mechanics.
- Ensure that correct technical skills are used when players are on the ball.
- Encourage players to use clear communication – visual and audio.

Sets and reps: 3 sets of 6 reps with 1 minute recovery between each set, i.e. 3 reps as player 1 and 3 reps as player 2.

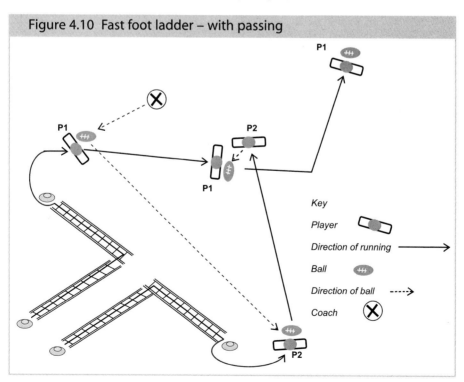

Figure 4.10 Fast foot ladder – with passing

Fast Foot Ladder – close contact grid

Aim: To develop fast feet, agility and control in a restricted area while under pressure from other players.

Description:

Place four ladders side by side. Working in pairs, players will work one on each of the outside ladders and perform Fast Foot drills while covering the length of the ladder. On a signal from the coach the players will move to the centre ladders, thus working side by side.

Key teaching points:

- Maintain correct running form/mechanics.
- Encourage players to push and nudge each other to simulate the close contact situations that occur in a game.
- If players are 'knocked' off balance, ensure they reassert the correct arm mechanics as soon as possible.
- On passing the ball ensure that the player reasserts the correct arm mechanics as soon as possible.

Sets and reps: 3 sets of 4 reps with 1 minute recovery between each set.

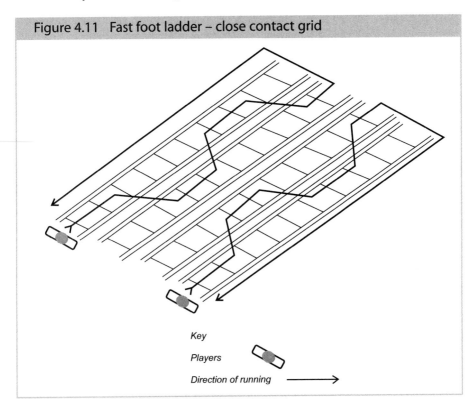

Figure 4.11 Fast foot ladder – close contact grid

Key

Players

Direction of running $\longrightarrow$

Fast Foot Ladder – giant crossover

Aim: To develop fast feet, speed, agility, co-ordination and visual reaction skills both with and without the ball.

Description:

Place four ladders in a cross formation with 25 m between the ladders in the centre area. Place a ball at the end of one ladder and another at the end of an adjacent ladder. Split the squad into four equal groups and locate them at the start of each ladder. Players accelerate down the ladder simultaneously performing Fast Foot drills. Two players will receive a ball at the end of their respective ladders, the ball being passed to them as they accelerate across the centre area. The player who has received the ball then pop-passes the ball to the oncoming player. Well-timed passes mean the ball will remain in the centre area. Having passed the ball the player joins the queue on the opposite side of the cross. Do not travel down this ladder.

Key teaching points:

- This should be a continuous drill.
- Maintain correct running form/mechanics.
- Ensure that correct technical skills are used when players are on the ball.
- Encourage players to use clear communication.

Sets and reps: 3 sets of 6 reps with 1 minute recovery between each set.

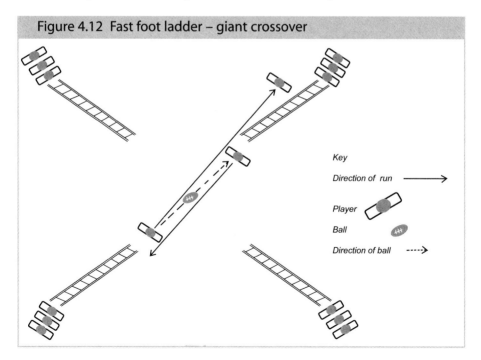

Figure 4.12 Fast foot ladder – giant crossover

Key

Direction of run   ⟶

Player

Ball

Direction of ball ⤏

Rugby-specific ladder drills

Two drills are detailed below which encourage players to improve their foot-work as well as developing technical proficiency in some core rugby skills.

Handling and realignment in attack

Rugby relevance – core handling skills through ladders and realignment.
Position relevance – all – particularly backs.

1. Set up the ladders as in the diagram.
2. Player 1 runs out, receives a pass from the scrum half and passes the ball to player 2, who has moved into his ladder, and so on until the ball is with player 4.
3. Having passed the ball, players complete their footwork through the ladder, sprint out of the ladder, around the cone directly in front, and then run backwards to the cone to the right of their ladder.
4. When player 4 receives the ball he continues through the ladder, sprints forward to the cone directly in front and then passes to player 3, who has realigned; the movement continues down the line until the ball is with player 1, who scores the try.

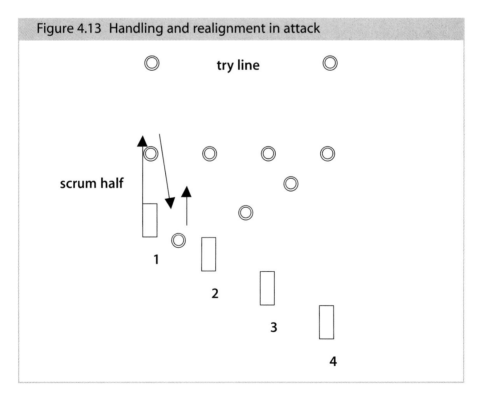

Figure 4.13 **Handling and realignment in attack**

Progressions:
- Add defender(s) for the players to beat once they have realigned.
- Change direction of sprint out of ladder so players practise realigning from different start positions.
- Change position of realignment cone so players have to come from different angles onto the ball.
- Adapt distances worked and have players wearing viper belts.

Footwork fend

Rugby relevance – fending off and change of direction.
Position relevance – all.

1. Set up the ladder as in the diagram.
2. Player runs out and performs footwork pattern through ladder.
3. On receiving a pass he fends off a defender holding a contact shield and sprints out to a designated cone as directed by the coach.
4. Defender is 2 m away from the ladder and moves towards the player as soon as the ball is passed.
5. Ensure that the fend is practised from both sides.

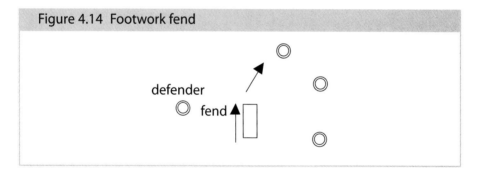

Figure 4.14 Footwork fend

Progressions:
- Add a defender on each side of the ladder so the player has to react to whichever defender confronts him and get the ball into the correct arm.
- Having fended out of the ladder, player then bursts through two defenders with shields 2 m away and ½ m apart.
- Add support players to offload to on fend.

Rugby-specific footwork patterns

Having developed a player's footwork skills through ladder work, it is then necessary to transfer this improvement into situations that occur during a game. This is necessary to ensure specific footwork patterns common to rugby are learned, and applied where it matters most – on the field.

The following footwork patterns are used when close to the contact area (within 2 m) where rapid ground contact is needed to unbalance defenders. This also provides maximum opportunity to drive off from the ground and to accelerate away with a change of direction.

3-step principle

Rugby relevance – footwork before contact to unbalance defenders.

1. Player sprints out and then follows the cone pattern.
2. Set out a red cone marked as a defender to provide the visual cue to the player (as a progression, swap the cone for a defender with a contact shield).
3. On approaching the red cone the player steps towards the space to move the defender.
4. Then back towards the defender to get the defender moving away from the area you want to attack (marked SPACE in the diagram).
5. With the defender now unbalanced, the player steps away from the defender for a third time towards the SPACE.
6. At this point put the ball in the hand furthest from the contact area (on the hip) so you can fend off a tackler.
7. Accelerate and repeat the footwork pattern through the undefended channel.
8. Perform the drill from both sides.

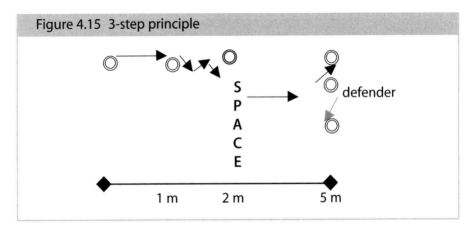

Figure 4.15 3-step principle

Progressions:
- Receive the ball while moving rather than starting off with it.
- Gather a rolling ball.
- Add a defender with a tackle shield to fend off.
- Add a support runner to 'leech'.
- Add two support runners to offload to when past the contact shield.
- Do ladder work before stepping to encourage quick feet and introduce combination ladder/skill work.
- Vary the start position to replicate game situations.

Spinning out of contact

Rugby relevance – footwork before/in contact to unbalance/avoid defenders.
Position relevance – all – particularly for runners off rucks or inside balls from scrum half or fly half.

1. Start at cone; sprint forwards on the balls of your feet.
2. Move out towards the defender with the contact shield with small quick steps to unbalance him and provide ground contact from which to change direction (the grey square in the diagram symbolises the defender).
3. Ensure that the steps are rapid, powerful and driving the player forward at pace rather than dancing from side to side.
4. Plant the right foot towards the defender's right shoulder, then rotate to your right off this foot, and spin away to go past defender on his left.
5. Sink at the hips to reduce the centre of gravity and to provide more power for the rotation. This takes place from the ball of the foot, and the heel does not touch the ground.
6. Repeat for both feet.

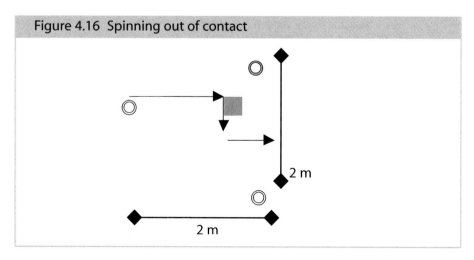

Figure 4.16 Spinning out of contact

2 m

2 m

Progressions:
- Vary start positions sideways and backwards from the ground before working on multiple ground contact.
- Approach start from walking, jogging, sprinting and jumping.
- Do ladder work before stepping to encourage quick feet and introduce combination ladder/skill work.
- Player to receive pass at different points of the movement.

Getting up

When a player is on the floor they are out of the game, so getting up as quickly and efficiently as possible is something that needs to be developed. The following drills look at how to propel the body up in one movement rather than walk the body up from the ground in stages. This is also very relevant in tackle situations; players should be encouraged to push up off the ground or opponent after making a tackle, and to be back on their feet as quickly as possible playing the ball.

Rebound get-up

Rugby relevance – reducing time spent on the floor and providing more powerful initial sprint start.
Position relevance – all.

Face down:
1. As if performing a press-up, push against the ground and force upper body up and backwards.
2. At the same time drive the dominant leg back against the ground to bring the lower body up and forwards. Swing the other leg forward under your body.
3. You should be on your feet in a single motion, leaning into your sprint.

Progressions:
- Practise this movement and then bring it into ladder drills, handling, shield-work and defensive drills, and any work that involves getting up from the floor.

On side:
1. Roll onto front.
2. Continue as for face down.

Sitting with back to opposition:

1. Push up with the arms in front of the shoulders and rotate your body 180 degrees, keeping dominant arm on the ground to do so. As the body rotates, move your arms so that when you have turned you are in a three-point sprint stance.
2. The dominant leg will be slightly further back, creating the correct position to drive off with contralateral arm action.
3. You should be on your feet in one motion, leaning forward into your sprint.

Ideally players will be able to push up and rotate on either arm straight onto their feet. Practise doing this from both sides with only one arm on the floor.

On back:

1. Sit up.
2. Continue as for sitting with back to opposition.

Sitting facing opposition:

1. Push with your arms slightly behind your hips and to the side; throw your legs back under your body until they are behind you.
2. At the same time drive your upper body up and forwards from your initial arm drive.
3. Your non-dominant arm will most likely remain on the floor and assist by acting as a point to rotate on; your dominant arm will provide the most force for this.
4. Your non-dominant leg will be furthest back with the non-dominant arm on the floor to make a three-point sprint stance.

Due to the force required to rotate around fully, most players will have to use their dominant arm, thus when they are in the three-point stance they will be driving from the less powerful leg. This is not ideal, but is preferable to trying to rotate on the non-dominant arm and being unable to do so, as this dramatically increases the time taken to get up and drive off.

Agility drills

These are some generic drills that cover core agility for rugby. Assessing the skills and movement patterns of specific positions will enable you to adapt these and design other drills to meet more positional-based needs.

X-run

Rugby relevance – turning, acceleration and deceleration.

1. Player sprints forwards 10 m from start, turns around the cone/pole, drives off the left foot and sprints 15 m across the grid.
2. Goes around cone/pole and runs forwards 10 m, turns around the cone/pole, drives off the right foot and sprints 15 m across the grid back to start.

Intensity: 100 per cent.
Reps: 5
Sets: 2–3
Recovery: 30 seconds between runs with 3 minutes between sets.

Figure 4.17 X-run

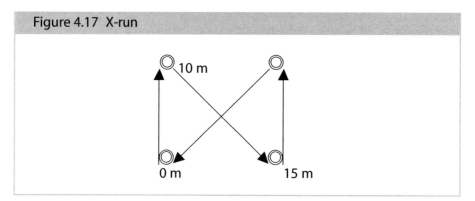

Progressions:
- Utilise different start positions and cues to begin run.
- Receive and give a pass in middle.
- Work in pairs and time run to perform switch in middle.
- Turn it into an overspeed and resistance drill using bungee cord.
- Set up two stations and have players race each other.

V and out

Rugby relevance – multi-directional running, acceleration, deceleration and footwork to unbalance defenders.

1. Player starts to the left, sprints 10 m forwards and around cone/pole.
2. Then runs backwards and around cone/pole at start.
3. Sprints forwards 5 m around cone/pole and steps through to the left or right channel as directed by the coach.
4. When performing second repetition start to the right of the start cone/pole.

Intensity: 100 per cent.
Reps: 5
Sets: 2–3
Recovery: 30 seconds between runs and 3 minutes between sets.

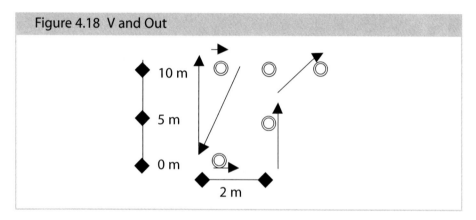

Figure 4.18 V and Out

Progressions:
• Utilise different start positions and cues to initiate run.
• Player to receive a pass as he/she approaches channel to attack.
• Add defender to step out and fill a channel for player to avoid.
• Add support runner after receiving pass.

Agility forest

Rugby relevance – turning, acceleration, deceleration and close-to-contact-area footwork.

1. Player sprints from the start into the work area (15 m × 15 m) and around all the poles in an order of their choice.
2. Then sprints away from last cone/pole through the finish gate.

Intensity: 100 per cent.
Reps: 5
Sets: 2–3
Recovery: 30 seconds recovery between runs and 3 minutes rest between sets.

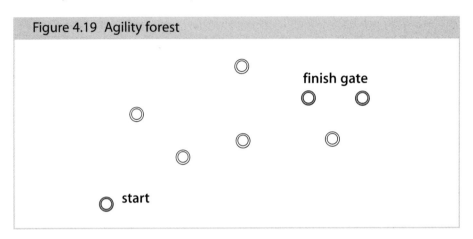

Figure 4.19 Agility forest

Progressions:
- Poles are numbered and the order is called by the coach as the player sprints out to work area.
- Add defender with shield as player leaves the work area for the player to beat to get through gate.

Hook in

Rugby relevance – evasion footwork in broken field – particularly for counter attack from kicks.

1. Player runs in wide arc as if running around chasers of a kick.
2. On reaching the yellow cone he steps in as if cutting across corner-flagging defender.
3. When he arrives at the last cone he decides if he straightens or cuts back towards the corner to score.
4. Perform from both sides and make 4–6 runs per set.

Intensity: 100 per cent.
Reps: 5
Sets: 2–3
Recovery: Walk back recovery plus 30 seconds and 3 minutes rest between sets.

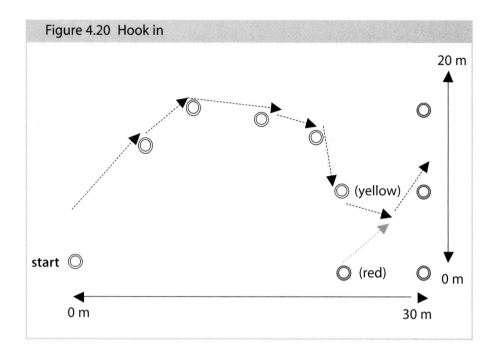

Figure 4.20 Hook in

Progressions:
- Player fields the ball then performs run while carrying it.
- Defenders are added to chase the kick and provide passive pressure to increase realism.
- Add a defender at the red cone who tries to prevent the attacker scoring; the defender leaves when the attacker gets round the last cone.
- Add more defenders and attackers to support.

Reactions

Reaction work needs to be included in sprint and agility training – the faster a player is able to react, the quicker he or she will be able to put the body into motion. Stimuli that occur in rugby should be used where possible to make this training more specific. To assist this, video analysis of opponents' (individual and team) movement patterns can help coaches and players identify the cues (stimuli) that may precede certain movements.

Reaction time

This is the time it takes from the presentation of a stimulus to the initiation of a response. For example, when a pass comes your way, the reaction time is the time it takes you to decide to catch the ball from the moment you first saw it. Choice reaction time is when there is more than one stimulus or response that the player has to choose from. For example, a pass comes your way and, because of pressure, alignment and height of the ball you decide not to catch and pass, but flick the ball on to a team-mate.

Reaction drills

T drops

Rugby relevance – reactions, acceleration, deceleration, defensive footwork, realignment and power.

1. Players are in pairs with one working and one resting.
2. Player A is working and is in a three-point stance 2 m away from player B, who has arms extended to each side at shoulder height with a tennis ball in each hand.
3. Player B drops a tennis ball from either hand and player A moves forward to catch the ball before it bounces twice.
4. Player A passes the ball back to player B and returns to the start position.
5. When the set is complete the players swap roles – this is the recovery time for player A.

Adjust the distance between the players based on age, ability and variation being used.

Intensity: 100 per cent.
Reps: 4–8 catches
Sets: 2–3
Recovery: Rest while partner works; 2 minutes between sets.

Progressions:

- On each effort, once the player has caught the ball the second ball is dropped and player A has to catch this ball as well.
- Utilise different start positions.
- Different stimulus ('Gone' or 'ball out' as would be called from ruck or scrum, or 'up 1, 2' for defensive cue).
- Start with back to partner or eyes closed – open them on verbal cue, which signals release of ball.
- Each time the ball is caught the dropper spins around and the catcher has to realign to be facing his partner, still 2 m away, before the next drop.
- Use a rugby ball and lob them up rather than dropping them.

This is a simple drill for acceleration and reaction training and is both enjoyable and competitive for the players.

Reaction race

Rugby relevance – acceleration, deceleration, turning and reactions.

1. Players race each other by sprinting out from start positions (A and B) and around their respective cone/pole.
2. The coach selects which cone the players must race to when they approach the turning gate and players sprint to get there first.

Intensity: 100 per cent.
Reps: 4–8
Sets: 2–3
Recovery: 30 seconds recovery between runs and three minutes rest between sets.

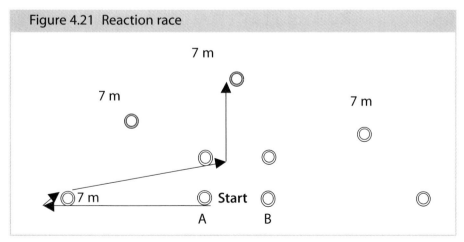

Figure 4.21 Reaction race

7 m

7 m

7 m

7 m

Start

A   B

Progressions:
- Select one of the players to decide which cone they will race to so one player has to react to the other.
- Utilise different start positions.

Field and pass

Rugby relevance – acceleration, deceleration, turning to field the ball and changing direction.

1. Player A stands 10 m from player B in a 10 × 10 m square and sprints forward.
2. When he is 5 m away, player B rolls or throws the ball to the side, in front or behind player A who reacts, fields the ball and passes back to player B.
3. Player A returns to the start position.

Intensity: 100 per cent.
Reps: 4–8
Sets: 2–3
Recovery: Walk-back recovery between repetitions and rest when throwing for partner.

Progressions:
- Utilise different start positions.
- Player A has to avoid a two-handed touch from partner, who has followed the ball, and try to leave the work area without being touched.
- Use balls of different sizes and weights to improve differentiation and weight of pass.

Speed/agility and LTAD

FUNdamental (6–8 years)

Basic movement patterns and mechanics should be introduced. Due to the physical state of development, short-duration (less than five seconds) activity such as agility runs are best employed to improve co-ordination and speed of movements. This needs to developed through game play, with the emphasis on fun and enjoyment.

Learning to train (9–11 years)

Physical changes mean that the body can now cope with longer bouts of high-intensity exercise (up to 20 seconds), and agility and speed training can be developed accordingly. Light hopping and bounding can be introduced, while game play should again be used to develop this, together with speed and agility.

Training to train (12–14 years)

Due to growth spurts, movement patterns need to be reinforced as players learn to cope with changes in their centre of gravity and limb length. This is the second window of opportunity to develop speed for maximal player development. Players are mentally more capable of understanding techniques, tactics and relevance of aspects of speed and agility for rugby. Speed, agility and co-ordination will develop rapidly during this phase.

Training to compete (15–17 years), learning to win and training to win (18 years+)

The full range of rugby-based speed training needs to be incorporated into a player's training programme.

Summary

These drills will provide you with a starting point from which to develop your own practices and sessions to improve speed and rugby-specific movements.

Speed and agility training is all about quality and recovery – ensure your sessions are based around this and you will begin to see results in the speed and movement patterns of your players. These primary methods of developing speed should be complemented by secondary methods such as strength/power training, flexibility and plyometrics to bring about maximal gains. It is vital that an appropriate warm-up and cool-down is carried out before and after each session to prevent injury and to aid recovery.

CHAPTER 5

Strength and power

Many rugby clubs have invested in weights rooms to encourage players to develop their strength and power to increase the physicality of their game. Tackling, lifting, scrummaging, winning collisions, mauling and wrestling for possession are some of the situations in which physical strength is critical for successful performance.

Players quite often follow an ad hoc training programme where they perform a random set of exercises that they have seen other people carrying out, often with no monitoring or progression of their training. They also perform 'beach weights' religiously, focusing on a couple of body parts to the exclusion of all others. This will improve physical appearance, but will have a limited benefit on rugby-specific strength and performance.

As with any form of training, it is vital that technique and basic movement are learned and perfected before increasing the difficulty of the exercise or the resistance. This is especially true when working with weights, due to the risk of injury that performing this type of training incorrectly can result in. Always consult a suitably qualified instructor before embarking on a resistance-based programme and develop safe practice, technique, stability and strength before attempting to develop power.

Strength, power and the young player (LTAD)

There is no definitive answer as to when a player should begin weight training. Children have individual rates of development – as such they can be the same age but be at significantly different stages of physical development. Only players who are mature beyond their chronological age should consider using resistance above their body weight before the age of 17. Body-weight resistance such as press-ups, dips and pull-ups are adequate strength development for those whose physical development is not ahead of their chronological age.

However, there is no reason why children cannot be taught the correct lifting techniques from a young age – a broomstick can replace the bar and the technique developed. This way, when they are physically mature enough to begin lifting they will already be competent with the movement patterns and will be able to make more rapid progress.

The most likely causes of injury for a young player carrying out a strength-training programme are exactly the same as for adults:

- poor technique
- unsupervised training where bad habits are not corrected
- lifting weights that are too heavy
- using apparatus inappropriate to their size.

Growth plates

As the bones are growing and forming they are more susceptible to damage as the newly forming cells are weaker than the surrounding bone. Damaging these cells can cause deformation of the limb or prevent further bone growth occurring. This is the main reason for opposition to young persons taking part in strength-training pro-grammes.

RFU guidelines for weight training for U17 players

1. Programmes must be devised and overseen by a suitably qualified instructor.
2. The player must be physically mature, probably in advance of his chronological age and playing at representative level.
3. Correct technique is of paramount importance and no weight should be used until the technique is correctly learned.
4. Moderate loadings should be used with high repetitions with the aim of developing muscular endurance (12–15 repetitions).
5. A mix of single-joint and multi-joint exercises should be used to work all the major muscle groups.

If there is any doubt about the readiness of a young player to undertake a strength-training programme, then err on the side of caution.

(Club England Fitness Team, 2000)

Developing strength and power

Strength is defined as the ability of a muscle or group of muscles to exert force to overcome a resistance, and is generally expressed in the weights room as a 1 rep max (the maximum weight you can perform once on a given exercise). Power is a combination of speed and strength – essentially, the quicker you can perform a strength-based action with control, the more powerful you are.

Rugby involves strength and power to be performed in a number of different ways during a game. There is static (isometric) strength when the muscles are contracting and tense but there is no movement around the joint. Maintaining a good scrummaging position or holding on to a ball in a maul are examples of this type of strength; this can be developed by applying resistance at a fixed angle. In rugby, static strength revolves around core stability/strength and wrestling/grappling activities. However, the majority of the muscle actions we perform when walking, running and jumping are isotonic – they have a concentric phase (the muscle contracts and shortens) and an eccentric phase (the muscle lengthens). Most weight training follows this principle with a weight being lowered or raised, causing the muscles working to produce more force to shorten or lengthen.

Principles of weight training

The principles of training are the same for any component of fitness – when attempting to develop strength and power it is particularly important to follow the following laws.

Overload

Muscles must be made to work beyond the level that they are accustomed to in order for any improvement from training to occur. In weight training this needs to be a progressive overload – once the muscles have adapted so they can cope with the weight being lifted, the weight needs to be increased in order to promote further adaptation and muscular improvement. Strength training does not result in more muscle fibres being produced; these numbers are genetically determined. Muscle fibres become thicker and stronger (hypertrophy) as a result of training, which accounts for the changes in size and muscular definition a person experiences.

Adaptation

The initial improvements from weight training are primarily due to intermuscular co-ordination (2–4 weeks) and then from adaptations in the neural pathway (6–8 weeks). This brings about an increase in the number of muscle fibres recruited during the exercise and the efficiency with which they are activated.

It is only after 10 weeks or more of regular weight training that muscle hypertrophy becomes apparent. The muscle fibres' greater size allows for more force to be applied during a single contraction.

Specificity

In order to make strength or power gains the appropriate forms of training need to be undertaken. Lifting light weights will not bring about the same strength gains as lifting heavy weights, thus training needs to be specific to your goals.

Reversibility

If the system of progressive overload is not followed then further gains will not be made. If training ceases then the gains will quickly be lost and the adaptations of muscle strength and size will reverse (atrophy).

Frequency

In order to bring about significant improvements in strength and power a programme of regular training needs to be undertaken. Individual experience and goals will determine the level and type of training, but three or four sessions should ideally be performed in the pre-season. This will maximise the gains made before other training demands reduce the time that can be devoted to strength and power development. In season, players should attempt to perform at least two sessions a week to maintain and develop the gains that the early season training has brought.

Muscle fibres

Muscle fibres are classified into two main categories based on the speed at which they contract: fast twitch and slow twitch. All muscle groups are made up of these different types of fibres – the percentage of the types you have are determined by genetics, but can be altered by the type of exercise you perform. Slow-twitch fibres are recruited first in any activity, and only if the load is great enough will the faster fibres be recruited. Thus in order to develop these fibres, training needs to performed with heavy loads in order to bring about maximal strength and power development.

Fast twitch

Type 2b: these are easily fatigued, but have a high capacity for anaerobic work and contract quicker than other fibre types, making them most desirable for strength, speed and power-based activities.

Type 2a: though not contracting with the same speed and force as type 2b fibres, these are largely responsible for the ability to produce strength and power. With power training these can begin to operate more like type 2b fibres.

Slow twitch

Type 1: these are highly resistant to fatigue and have a large capacity for aerobic metabolism, which makes them ideal for endurance-based activity.

Recovery

When performing resistance training, suitable recovery periods need to be observed between workouts in order for adaptation and recovery to take place. When first undertaking such a programme, players will require two or three days in order to fully recover from their exertions. The body will quickly become used to the training and anything between 24 and 48 hours is generally a sufficient period of rest before commencing the next training session. Having three or four days rest included at points in the training year, particularly after a period of intense training, will not cause atrophy or detraining to occur. It may actually be beneficial both mentally and physically to the player to have these breaks in training to allow them to resume the next cycle renewed and refreshed.

How to train strength and power for rugby

When you think of weight training you immediately visualise a room with lots of machines and the traditional exercises such as bicep curls, bench presses, leg extensions and so on. Many of these exercises isolate single muscle groups in order to place them under strain to facilitate strength gains. All of these exercises will result in improved strength and size if performed properly, with the correct frequency and progressive overload.

Now think of a game of rugby – when do you perform a bicep curl, bench press or leg extension during the course of a game? When do you only work one particular muscle group in isolation from all others in the body? You need the strength that these exercises bring to these body parts, but how functional are they to the actions that are performed on the pitch? A lot of these exercises are performed sitting or lying down and as such do not represent the way that strength needs to be applied during the game, that is standing on your feet. These exercises should have a place in strength training, but there are ways to train that will enable a greater degree of transfer into sporting situations. It makes sense to train in a way that best reflects the demands of the sport.

Functional training

Functional training essentially promotes multi-joint activity, and by training in this way players have to develop balance, stability and joint co-ordination, and manage their body weight while performing an exercise. These are all required while performing any rugby-based skill, so training to develop strength in this way will have an increased benefit on performance over single-joint exercises. Most functional exercises are performed standing with the feet in contact with the ground (closed chain) to reflect the demands of the sport and the fact that the body, not a machine, needs to provide stability while performing an action. There are many occasions in sport when the body is in an unstable position and the athlete needs to be able to control this. Functional training reflects this need and encourages the progression of certain exercises to an unstable surface, such as using one leg, jelly discs or foam pads to stand on.

As much as possible, exercises that reflect the demands of the sport should be used to develop strength. Functional training is an excellent means of achieving this and will develop strength and improvements in balance and co-ordination that traditional isolation training cannot. This will also help reduce the risk of injury as players develop better body control.

Weight room terminology

Free weights and machines

Free weights are much more supportive of the concept of functional training than machines. Machine-based resistance training generally isolates a particular muscle group to be worked – by providing stability machines remove the actions of stabiliser muscles acting around the joint. These machines are safer and are beneficial when working alone or developing confidence in inexperienced trainers.

Percentage of 1 rep max (1RM)

A 1 rep max is the maximum weight that can be successfully lifted with control and good technical execution. This is then used to calculate the weight that should be lifted for that exercise and the number of repetitions and sets, dependent upon the desired training goals.

Repetitions

This is the number of times you perform an exercise or lift. Lifting lighter weights with more repetitions (15–20) brings about greater improvements in muscular endurance. The heavier the weight that is lifted, the fewer the number of repetitions that are performed, and the greater the benefits in strength development.

Sets

This is the number of times you perform the repetitions.

Recovery/rest time

This is the time taken between completing one set and starting the next. The greater the weight being lifted, the longer the recovery time that is needed in order to allow for the maximum number of muscle fibres to be recruited for the next set. Failing to allow an adequate recovery period reduces the effectiveness of the training and the degree of adaptation that occurs.

Table 5.1 General guidelines for weight training

Training for	Sets	Reps	% 1RM	Recovery time
Power	3–5	1–6	85–100	3–5 min
Strength	3	6–12	70–80	2–3 min
Muscular endurance	3	15–20	50–60	45–90 sec

Supersetting

This can take on two forms. First, to perform exercises that work the same muscle group directly after the other with no rest period, e.g. bench press followed directly by dumbbell flye. This is highly fatiguing and so would result in a lower weight being lifted due to the lack of a recovery period between exercises. Second, to work opposing muscle groups in the same manner, e.g. bench press followed directly by bent-over row. This is a popular method of training as it means more exercises/sets can be performed in a short period of time.

Pyramids

In this form of training the weight begins heavy and a low number of repetitions are performed; the weight is then decreased and a higher number of repetitions are performed. This can be performed starting from low weight to high with the repetitions being decreased. For strength gains, the heavy to light approach allows for greater improvement as the muscles are not fatigued when they come to perform the heavier lifts.

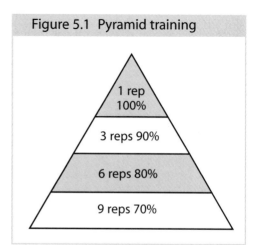

Figure 5.1 Pyramid training

1 rep 100%

3 reps 90%

6 reps 80%

9 reps 70%

Tempo

This relates to the speed at which the exercise is performed and describes the movement speed at the different stages of execution, e.g. squat – tempo 2, 0, 2. This means the weight is lowered for a count of 2 until the thighs are parallel and then returned back up for a count of 2. Power lifts are performed explosively to encourage Rate of Force Development (RFD – see below), and tempos can be varied depending on the exercise and the desired training outcome.

Breathing

As a rule players should breathe in and contract the core muscles to provide a stable base before initiating a lift, then exhale on the effort phase.

Why develop power?

Once a player has developed a good strength base with sound technical execution they should look to develop this into explosive power. Strength training is important to rugby, but power is the key that unlocks the door to releasing a player's athletic potential. Rugby is a sport that is made up of collisions and contacts, when strength needs to be applied at speed in order to make a tackle, break a tackle, clear a ruck or lift a jumper.

Power = Speed × Strength

To develop power, the speed at which strength is applied is critical. This is referred to as the Rate of Force Development (RFD) – the greater the RFD of an individual, the more power they can produce. The RFD in strength training is slow and as such does not transfer into power that can be applied in a game, therefore in order to bring about improvements training needs to target RFD.

England Conditioning Coach, Dave Reddin, believes that the power benefits associated with using light weights to facilitate greater speed of movement result more in muscular co-ordination improvements than increases in the muscular force development. Power training requires RFD to be increased – the weight used needs to be high in order to recruit as many muscle fibres as possible and to specifically target the fibres that can produce the greatest force (type 2b muscle fibres). Whereas the muscles are forced to contract very quickly in order to reach their peak force, it is the speed of the muscle contraction – not the speed at which the weight is lifted – that is the key to power development.

Power training for rugby is required for one-off actions such as tackling or lifting, but due to the nature of the game a player will be required to make a number of powerful movements in one passage of play. It is therefore necessary to ensure that power training reflects this and is not solely focused on one-off maximal lifts.

Power training is dependent upon quality and intensity rather than quantity. Training without these principles and without long rest periods will not bring about the desired improvements in power production. Power lifts should be performed at the beginning of a weights session, after a suitable warm-up and stretching and before the body is fatigued, for maximum benefit and safety. Fatiguing core exercises should not be performed before these lifts for the same reason.

There is a fear that by carrying out power training players will put on weight and will be unable to move around the pitch. However, this is not the case, as power training will increase speed, acceleration and explosive movement – which is why it is such a major part of sprint training programmes. Performing such multi-joint activities will also make players more resistant to the rotational and lateral forces they will experience in a game, therefore reducing the risk of injury.

Complex and contrast training

This method of training couples strength training with a plyometric-based exercise in order to recruit more muscle fibres and therefore improve RFD. It is also a more functional way of training as the exercises will have a greater relevance to actions carried out on the pitch. A resistance exercise for a specific muscle group is performed and then a plyometric exercise for this muscle group follows. The resistance exercise provides an initial stimulus that activates motor units and muscle fibres. As a result the neural system is in a state of readiness, leading to greater recruitment of muscle fibres in the following plyometric exercise. For example, bench press is followed by drop press-ups, back squat is followed by box squat jumps, lunge is followed by single leg hops. The player would complete all of the prescribed sets of the resistance exercise before moving on to the plyometric exercise.

Contrast training works on the same principle, except that the resistance and plyometric exercises are performed as a superset. The resistance exercise is performed and then, after a minute to a minute and a half's rest period, the plyometric exercise is performed. This is a high-intensity form of training and should not be attempted until a base level of strength has been established.

Take 3–5 minutes rest between the superset exercises and before commencing the next superset.

Table 5.2 Examples of matched exercises of complex/contrast training

Exercise	Sets	Reps	% 1RM	Recovery time
Bench press	3	6	85	2–4 min
Drop push-ups	3	6		
Squats	3	6	85	2–4 min
Box squat jumps	3	6		
Lunge	3	6	85	2–4 min
Single leg bounds	3	6		

Strength and power exercises for rugby

The rugby season is not best suited for developing strength and power gains. There is only a short period out of competition when this component of rugby fitness can receive the required attention. In season, playing and recovering from games and the time constraints on the individual and the team mean that gains made during the off season are often at best only maintained during the season. As a result, developing strength and power takes a number of years of planned training in order to cope with the difficulties that the structure of the rugby season presents.

Programmes need to contain a mix of pushing and pulling exercises, working all the major muscle groups to prevent imbalances that can result in injury. The following exercises are appropriate for inclusion in a rugby player's training programme and, with the correct planning and prescription, will help to bring about strength and power gains.

Safety and weight training
- All programmes should be prescribed by a suitably qualified trainer, with technical execution taking precedence over the amount of weight lifted.
- Exercises should be performed with body weight as resistance to facilitate the above, before gradually increasing the external load or instability.
- Assess individual lifting competence, experience, strengths and weaknesses when designing a programme.
- Wear appropriate clothing and footwear, and train in an appropriate environment with the correct equipment. Check all equipment before use for faults or damage.
- Always use collars to secure weights in place and work with spotters when using free weights.
- Carry out a suitable warm-up and cool-down.

- If you experience pain when lifting, stop exercising, visit the medical staff and have your trainer review your technique.

Olympic lifts

Power clean

This is a core exercise for the development of total body power and requires the co-ordination of all the major muscle groups. This is not an exercise that should be attempted until a high degree of lifting competence has been achieved, and should be broken down and taught in stages by a qualified instructor before performing the exercise with any significant load.

Muscles targeted: gluteals, quadriceps, hamstrings, deltoids and trapezius.

Description:

1. **'Get set'** – address the bar with the feet hip width apart, squat down and take the bar with an overhand grip slightly further than shoulder width apart. Hips must be higher than the knees and the shoulders higher than the hips; keep the chest up, back flat and look directly ahead.

2. **'First pull'** – breathe in and contract the abdominal and lower back muscles, then lift the bar up as powerfully as you can by driving up, extending the knees and moving the hips forward so the bar is just below the knees; the back must be kept flat.

3. **'Scoop'** – when the bar is brought over the knees the hips are then thrust forwards and up, and the torso extended.

4. **'Second Pull'** – bring the bar up, brushing the thighs, continuing the powerful hip movement and extending the ankles. Shrug the shoulders and bend the elbows, pulling the bar up as high as possible and keeping the elbows above the wrists.

5. **'Catch'** – rotate the elbows so they are under the bar and pointing forwards. Flex the knees and hips slightly to absorb the weight and finish with the bar resting on the front of the shoulders.

Progressions/variations:

This exercise can be performed from a hang position (bar at thigh height) to develop the later part of the lift or to concentrate on the upper body to a greater degree. Having performed the power clean, the bar could be pressed above the head to develop the exercise into a clean and press.

Snatch

This exercise develops whole body power and, once the correct technique is learned, will help to bring about significant gains. It is not an exercise that should be attempted until a high degree of lifting competence has been achieved, and should be broken down and taught in stages by a qualified instructor before the exercise is performed with any significant load.

Muscles targeted: gluteals, quadriceps, hamstrings, deltoids and trapezius.

Description:
1. Address the bar with the feet hip width apart, squat down and take the bar with an overhand grip with the hands further apart than for the power clean. The hips must be higher than the knees and the shoulders higher than the hips; keep the chest up, back flat and look directly ahead.
2. Breathe in and contract the abdominal and lower back muscles, then lift the bar up as powerfully as you can by driving up, extending the knees and moving the hips forward so the bar is just below the knees; the back must be kept flat.
3. When the bar is brought over the knees, the hips are then thrust forwards and up and the torso extended.

4. Bring the bar up, brushing the thighs, continuing the powerful hip movement and extending the ankles. Shrug the shoulders and bend the elbows, pulling the bar up as high as possible, keeping the elbows above the wrists.

5. As the bar comes up to the head, the pull is continued and the arms extended to finish with the arms locked and the bar above the head. The lifter will drop down into a squat position at the same time before standing up to complete the lift.

Progressions/variations:
Due to the difficulty of this exercise it is easier for many to perform a split-leg (see photo) as opposed to a squat-style snatch. This exercise can also be performed from a hang position (bar at thigh height) to develop the later part of the lift. The wider hand grip allows for greater weight to be lifted, but the exercise can also be performed from shoulder width as a means of developing the technique.

Clean and jerk

This Olympic lift is a combination of the power clean and the push press, the jerk phase generally being performed with a split squat to make the lift easier. Although this is a complex movement pattern, the strength and power benefits of such a lift are great.

Muscles targeted: gluteals, quadriceps, hamstrings, deltoids, pectorals and trapezius.

Description:
1. The technique for the power clean is followed; from the finish position the lifter pushes the bar above his head and completes the lift with the arms fully extended and the bar above the head.
2. This requires the lifter to bend the knees and squat down slightly, then drive up pushing the bar above the head, extending the ankles, knees and hips at the same time. Look ahead throughout the exercise to achieve this finish position, maintaining a flat back.
3. As the bar is driven up, the lifter splits the legs, sending one backwards, finishing in a split squat with the bar above the head.

Progressions/variations:
A powerbag can be used to perform the exercise with a jerk/throw to further add to the dynamic nature of the exercise.

Power lifting exercises

Back squat

This exercise is the cornerstone of any strength and power programme as it is a multi-joint exercise targeting the muscles that extend the knee and hip. It is often poorly performed with excessive weights, which limits its effectiveness and can lead to injury. Players frequently load the bar but do not perform an appropriate range of movement (ROM) – it is critical to utilise a good ROM in order to fully derive the benefits of this exercise. Players may need to carry out flexibility work in order to achieve this and should reduce the weight lifted (or perform body-weight squats) to ensure they work the correct range.

Muscles targeted: quadriceps, gluteals, hamstrings, adductors, spinal erectors (lower back) and abdominals.

Description:
1. In a squat rack, stand with the bar across the upper back (not the neck) with the feet slightly further than shoulder width apart; the toes can be angled fractionally outwards.
2. Grip the bar in an overhand position (knuckles facing up) just over shoulder width apart.
3. Looking directly ahead, lower the bar by flexing the hips and knees, keeping the chest high and the back flat. The knees should not come forward past the toes, the heels should remain on the floor and the weight should be felt over the ankle rather than on the toes.

4. Lower the bar until the thighs are parallel with the ground. Push up by forcing the heels into the floor, bringing the hips forward and keeping the chest high and the back flat.

Players with poor flexibility at the ankle, knee or hip joint can squat with a platform under the heels to enable them to perform a deeper squat. This may place excessive force on the knee joint, but provided the knee does not go past the toes then this should not be the case (this practice should be carefully monitored).

Progressions/variations:

Front squats – the bar is positioned across the front of the shoulders (anterior deltoid) and held in the finish position for the power clean with the elbows pointing forward and the wrists extended. Some players will find this grip uncomfortable and can use a crossed-arm grip instead. This exercise targets the quadriceps to a greater extent and you should use less weight than when performing back squats.

Bench press

This is probably the exercise that carries the most kudos with rugby players as it is commonly used to provide an indicator of upper body strength. Quite often, improvements in this exercise are pursued at the expense of all others, which has implications in terms of muscle imbalance. In terms of rugby it is not particularly functional as it is performed lying down – the push-up is a more functional exercise for the upper body.

Muscles targeted: pectorals, triceps, deltoids and serratus.

Description:

1. Lie flat on the bench, with the shoulder blades and buttocks in contact with the bench and the feet on the ground.
2. There will naturally be a slight gap between the bench and the lower back, which should not increase during the exercise.
3. Hold the bar with an overhand grip of medium width.
4. Lower the bar to the chest at about the nipple line, with the elbows at 4 and 8 o'clock positions.
5. The wrist should be kept straight with the knuckles facing directly to the ceiling to reduce stress on this joint.
6. Push up away from the chest and slightly back towards the shoulders to return the bar to the start position.

Progressions/variations:

Barbell/dumbbell/powerbag incline press – angle the bench up between 45 and 60 degrees and perform the pressing action as described above, but bring the bar down to the top of the chest. This targets the upper chest (pectorals) to a greater extent.

Barbell/dumbbell/powerbag decline press – angle the bench down between 20 and 40 degrees and perform the pressing action as described above, but bring the bar down to the bottom of the chest. This targets the lower chest (pectorals) to a greater extent. Make sure the feet are on the ground or anchored to prevent slipping and excessive movement during the lift.

The bench press can be performed on a Swiss ball (ensure the ball is suitable to carry this load) to bring in a greater degree of balance and stability work.

Deadlift

This lift is performed in power-lifting competitions as it recruits almost every major muscle during its execution and is therefore an excellent indicator of total body strength and power.

Muscles targeted: gluteals, hips, quadriceps, lower back and trapezius.

Description:
1. Address the bar with the feet hip width apart, squat down and grip the bar with an overhand grip, slightly wider than shoulder width apart. Keep the chest up and look directly ahead.
2. Breathe in and contract the abdominal and lower back muscles, then lift the bar by driving up, extending the knees and moving the hips forward.
3. As the bar is brought up to the knees, extend the torso so you are fully upright, making sure the back does not become rounded during the exercise.
4. Keep the bar as close to the body as you can throughout the exercise and keep the arms fully extended.

Progressions/variations:
An over-and-under grip can be used (one palm facing forwards, the other facing back) depending on personal preference.

More strength and power exercises for rugby

Lunge

This is an important exercise as it primarily targets the gluteals and quadriceps, and its multi-joint recruitment makes it highly functional.

Muscles targeted: gluteals, quadriceps, hamstrings and hip flexors.

Description:

1. In a squat rack, position the barbell across the back as if you were performing a back squat, using an overhand grip.
2. Stand with the feet shoulder width apart and take a step forward with the right leg, keeping the head up and the chest high throughout the exercise.
3. The knee of the right leg should be over the ankle (it should not go out past the toes); drop the hips to lower the thigh until it is parallel to the ground. Your weight will be placed over the right leg with the left knee slightly above the ground.
4. Push back off the right leg to return to the start position.
5. Perform the required number of repetitions for each leg, or alternate between them.

Variations/progressions:

Lunges can be performed backwards, diagonally and laterally to alter the way in which the muscles are recruited to work.

High pull

With little or no weight this is an excellent warm-up exercise. With the weight increased it is highly functional and a good whole-body strength developer. It is also a good way of learning the lifting technique used in the Olympic lifts such as the power clean.

Muscles targeted: quadriceps, hip flexors, hamstrings, trapezius and deltoids.

Description:

1. Address the bar with the feet hip-width apart, squat down and grip the bar with an overhand grip slightly wider than shoulder width apart. Keep the chest up and look directly ahead ('get set' position).
2. Keep the bar as close to the body as possible throughout the exercise. Initiate the first pull by driving up, extending the knees and moving the hips forward, lifting the shoulders in time with this ('first pull').
3. As the bar moves up the thigh you will be almost fully upright with the chest high and looking directly ahead ('scoop').
4. Continue to pull the bar up with explosive power by driving up onto the balls of the feet, extending the ankle, knee and hip joints. Maintain this upwards movement by shrugging the shoulders and drawing the shoulder blades in until the elbows are at shoulder height ('second pull').
6. Return to the start position in a controlled movement, maintaining a flat back.

Progressions/variations:

This can be performed from a hang position as an exercise in its own right or to develop the learning stage of the exercise. Taking a wider grip will help to develop the technique used for performing the snatch.

Bent-over row

This exercise is an excellent strength builder for the back and is a core strength exercise for rugby.

Muscles targeted: latissimus dorsi, teres (major/minor), deltoids, rhomboid, trapezius, infraspinatus, supraspinatus, biceps and brachialis.

Description:

1. Stand with the feet shoulder width apart with the knees slightly bent.
2. The upper body is bent forward while maintaining a flat back.
3. The hands are positioned more than shoulder width apart and the bar is grasped with an overhand grip, with the arms fully extended and the bar just below the knees.
4. Breathe in, contract the abdominals and pull the bar up to the stomach, keeping the head and shoulders up.
5. Extend the arms to return the bar to the start position.

113

Progressions/variations:
Altering the type and width of grip will bring a different slant to the exercise.

One-arm dumbbell row

This develops strength in the back muscles in much the same way as the bent-over row but through a single arm exercise.

Muscles targeted: latissimus dorsi, teres (major), deltoids, rhomboid, trapezius, biceps, brachioradialis and brachialis

Description:
1. Place one hand onto a bench and hold a dumbbell in the other hand with the palm facing inwards.
2. The back should be flat and the arm holding the dumbbell fully extended.
3. Pull the dumbbell up to the side of your body by bringing the shoulder blade in and pulling the elbow back as far as possible.
4. Breathe out as you complete the movement and lower the weight to the start position.

Progressions/variations:
Cheating rows – perform the exercise as described above, but as the dumbbell is brought up rotate the chest up and to the side to bring a rotational aspect to the exercise.

One arm one leg row – this is a highly functional exercise that, while performing a rowing pull, also requires a great degree of stabilisation from the ankle, knee and hip. At first stability will be difficult and the weight lifted quite light. Hold a low cable pulley with the left hand, stand on the right leg with the knee slightly bent and pull the cable back and to the side of the body. The height at which the cable is positioned can be adjusted to change the angle of the pull.

Push press

This is a very good multi-joint exercise that develops overall body strength and power as well as developing some of the lifting principles for the clean and press, and other power lifts.

Muscles targeted: gluteals, quadriceps, hamstrings, deltoids, pectorals and trapezius.

Description:
1. Stand with the feet roughly shoulder width apart with the knees slightly bent.
2. Rest the bar across the top of the chest with an overhand grip and the palms facing away from the body, slightly more than shoulder width apart.
3. Bend the knees, squat down slightly and drive up, pushing the bar above the head and extending the ankles, knees and hips as you drive up. Look ahead throughout the exercise to achieve the finish position, maintaining a flat back.
4. Finish with the bar above the head and the knees slightly bent; lower the weight with control back to the start position. Be sure to avoid hyperextending the back when performing this exercise.

Progressions/variations:
As the bar is pressed up the lifter can adopt a split-leg position to perform the jerk phase of the clean and jerk. Powerbags offer a good variation to the exercise and a push press can be developed into a push/throw to increase dynamic body movement.

Working with body weight

Push-ups

This is an excellent strength-development exercise and also requires core strength and stabilisation.

Muscles targeted: pectorals, triceps and deltoids.

Description:
1. Start with the body extended and the palms of the hands flat on the floor slightly more than shoulder width apart.
2. The feet should be close together with the head in line with the spine.
3. Push yourself up, extending the arms and keeping the body flat and the spine in line.
4. Lower yourself to the starting position and repeat.

Progressions/variations:
Elevate the feet to work the upper pectorals to a greater degree and elevate the hands to concentrate on the lower pectorals. An unstable surface can be added to increase the difficulty and a weight can be placed upon the upper back for external resistance.

Dips

These are used for upper-body strength development, and also help to improve the flexibility of the chest. Young players should perform this with their feet on the floor and their hands on a bench until they are ready to progress to the full dips.

Muscles targeted: deltoids, pectorals and triceps.

Description:
1. Grip the handles and lift the feet off the ground, bend the knees and cross the feet.

2. Lower the body by bending the elbows so that the elbows are above the shoulders, or as far as is comfortable. Your body will lean slightly forward as you do so.

3. Push up, extending the elbows to return to the start position.

Progressions/variations:
Leaning further forward works the pectorals to a greater degree and the straighter you are the more you work the triceps. Weight can be hung between the legs from a weights belt to increase the resistance.

Chin-ups

This works the back and arm muscles and indicates the ability of players to manage their body weight. While all players should be able to lift their own body weight, many players focus on pushing exercises for the chest rather than balancing this with pulling exercises for the back. Players who are unable to perform a pull-up can receive assistance from a spotter to enable them to perform the exercise.

Muscles targeted: latissimus dorsi, trapezius, rhomboids, teres, brachialis, brachioradialis and biceps brachii.

Description:
1. Grip the chin-up bar with an underhand grip, with the hands slightly more than shoulder width apart (stand on a box to do so).

2. Lower your body, extend the arms and then pull up so that the chin is lifted above the bar, keeping the body as still as possible during the movement.

Progressions/variations:
Weight can be hung between the legs from a weights belt to increase resistance. A more difficult variation is to pull the chest up to touch the bar instead of bringing up the chin; this requires a greater range of motion.

Pull-ups

This is a more difficult exercise as the change in grip and width means the arms are used less and more force is required from the back muscles.

Muscles targeted: latissimus dorsi, trapezius, rhomboids, teres, brachialis, brachioradialis and biceps brachii.

Description:
1. Grip the chin-up bar with a wide overhand grip (stand on a box to do so).
2. Lower your body, extend the arms and then pull up so that the eyes are lifted level with the bar, keeping the body as still as possible during the movement.

Progressions/variations:
Using different grips and widths of hand placement alters the nature of the exercise and targets the worked muscles in a slightly different manner.

Plyometric training

By introducing plyometric training into a power-based programme you will develop greater gains than by weight training alone. This is a particularly demanding form of training and should only be attempted by well-conditioned athletes with a good strength base. The training places the joints, bones and muscles under great strain and so the infrequent trainer, and children/teenagers who are still growing, should not perform this type of training.

Plyometric exercises require the muscles to perform an eccentric contraction (contract and lengthen) at high speed to recruit the fast-twitch fibres in large numbers. This eccentric phase occurs when the muscle is working against gravity and is used as a braking mechanism to slow the body or limb down. This results in greater tension and force production in the muscle, and is then immediately followed by a concentric contraction (muscles contract and shorten) that propels you away from the ground. Often referred to as the stretch–shortening cycle.

Basic rules for plyometric training

1. Be physically ready to cope with the demands of this type of training.
2. Players should be able to squat $1\frac{1}{2}$ times their body weight before undertaking the more intense forms of plyometrics.

3. Perform the activity on an appropriate surface – grass is one of the best surfaces for performing plyometric training.
4. Wear footwear that provides appropriate support.
5. Land with a locked ankle and with at least two-thirds of the foot in contact with the ground, with the weight on the front of the foot.
6. Perform a thorough warm-up and cool-down at the beginning and end of each session.
7. Technique is critical and sessions should be short, with long recovery periods, due to the intensity of the exercises and the effect fatigue will have on performance.
8. Allow at least 48 hours between plyometric sessions for the body to recover.

Plyometrics for rugby

Some plyometric exercises are detailed below – they can be used to devise a specific session or can be incorporated into a weights or rugby training session. As a basic guide 3–10 repetitions and 2 or 3 sets of the exercise (4–6 exercises per session) should be performed, depending on the training aims and level of difficulty. Start gradually and build up the volume of work, but remember it is the intensity and quality of work that is important. As soon as a player is showing signs of fatigue there is no point in continuing, as the benefits will be minimal and the players will be more disposed to injury. Recovery times between sets of between 2 and 3 minutes is generally sufficient, but this can be increased or reduced depending on the difficulty of the exercise.

Single (SR) and multiple response (MR)

This refers to whether the end of a plyometric movement is immediately followed by another movement on its completion or landing (MR), or if there is a pause before the next repetition (SR).

Single-response exercises require one powerful movement, for example jumps or throws. Multiple-response exercises require more co-ordination as the movement needs to be repeated immediately.

When first performing these exercises, pause between jumps (SR) to ensure you are landing correctly. Once you are competent, carry out the jumps with as little delay as possible between landing and jumping up again (MR).

Squat jump

Aim: to develop leg and hip power.

Stand with feet apart and your hands linked behind your head. Lower yourself into a half squat, stop the movement and immediately explode up as high as possible. As a variation, jump onto a box.

Tuck jump

Aim: to develop leg and hip power.

Stand with feet apart and hands across the chest with the palms facing down to the ground. Lower yourself into a quarter squat, stop this movement and immediately explode up as high as possible, trying to touch the palms of your hand with your knees. When first performing this exercise, pause between jumps (SR) to ensure you are landing correctly. Once you are competent, carry out the jumps with as little delay as possible between landing and jumping up again (MR).

Depth jump

Aim: to develop leg and hip power.

Stand on a box or bench with the front half of your feet hanging over the edge. Let yourself fall forwards off the box (do not jump), bringing your arms slightly behind and flexing the knees and hips to prepare for the take-off phase of the exercise. Immediately upon landing, drive the arms up and in front of the body and propel the body up, trying to gain as much height as possible.

Lateral box jump

Aim: to develop leg and hip power.

Stand with your left foot on the box and your right foot on the floor. Propel your arms forward in front of your body, drive off the box with the left foot and jump as high as possible while moving across the box so that the left leg lands

on the ground to the left side of the box. The right leg will land on the box and, as soon as the feet have landed, the next jump is initiated with the right leg driving up from the box.

Hurdle box jump

Aim: to develop leg and hip power.

Set up some hurdles, boxes, cones or tackle shields so that they are about a metre apart; the obstacles to be cleared should not be too high as the object is to clear them safely. Stand in front of the first box with the arms bent at the sides, squat slightly and drive up, bringing the arms forward as you jump over the hurdle going for maximal height; the knees should be tucked up to the chest. Landing should be done with full foot contact and with the knees slightly bent. At first perform this exercise with a pause between landing and jumping. When players can land successfully, attempt to minimise the ground contact time between jumps.

Bounding

Aim: to develop leg and hip power.

This exercise can be performed from a stationary, walking, jogging or running start. Push off from the rear leg, driving the knee up and through and trying to gain as much height and distance as possible. Use a contralateral arm swing (arm working with opposite leg) as you would do when running.

Once you have got used to landing comfortably on the same leg you took off on, with the knee slightly bent and the foot flat and directly under the hip, the exercise can be progressed into MR by alternating the leg action.

Lateral bound

Aim: to develop leg and hip power.

Squat down with the arms in front of the body, shift your weight onto the outside leg and drive off, aiming for distance not vertical height. The inside foot will land first and then the drive leg.

This can be progressed into a MR exercise with forward and lateral movements by setting out a course of cones for the player to jump to in turn. This type of exercise is excellent for developing explosive changes of direction and sidestepping. These sidesteps can then be followed by a short sprint to make the movement more rugby-specific.

Tackling dumbbell arm swing

Aim: to develop upper body power.

Stand with a dumbbell (less than 10 kg) in your right hand extended out in front of you, with the left hand supporting it. Your legs should be slightly more than shoulder width apart, with the right leg in front of the left. Bring the dumbbell back slightly behind the shoulder and bend the knees so you are in a semi-squat. Rotating from the hip and driving from the shoulder and chest, swing the dumbbell back to the start position keeping the elbow bent, and rise out off the squat, stepping the left leg forward as you perform the action. Catch the weight with your left arm and repeat for the desired number of repetitions, then swap sides.

Drop push-up

Aim: to develop upper-body power.

Assume a push-up position on two raised platforms and drop the hands off the boxes onto the floor. Soften the landing by bending the elbows and then push up immediately to return to the start position.

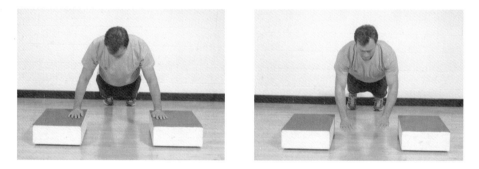

The throwing drills described in Chapter 7 can also be performed as plyometric exercises by ensuring that a stretch is initiated prior to the throw.

Progressing strength and power training

Table 5.3 provides some basic guidance on the way in which strength and power training can be structured and progressed. This is highly dependent upon individual growth, development, commitment and competence. The rate of players' progress will vary greatly and it can take a number of years of regular and continuous training to become an advanced lifter.

Table 5.3 Progressing strength and power training

Training principles	Stages of development			
	Players U17	17+ or novice	Intermediate	Advanced
Type of training	• Body-weight resistance. • Circuit training. • Technical development of lifting with free weights and machines.	• Body-weight resistance. • Circuit training. • Progressive overload with external resistance. • Technical development of lifting with free weights and power lifts.	• Hypertrophy and strength training cycles. • Power training cycles. • Multi-joint exercise should make up the bulk of the training and some instability progressions should be gradually developed. • Power lifts should be incorporated into training following technical competence and development of strength base. • Plyometric training should be introduced with the aim to develop competence in its execution.	• Training should be highly functional and specific to individual needs. • Maximal power and strength should be developed through well-planned training cycles. • Power lifts should be well learned. • Plyometric and complex training should form a part of this programme which, due to the player's competence and fitness levels, can be highly demanding and varied. • Resistance training with instability should be used regularly.
Frequency of training	1–3 (max) sessions/week	2–3 sessions/week	2–4 sessions/week	3–4 sessions/week
Volume of training	6–8 exercises (including core and abdominal) with 12–15 repetitions performing 2–3 sets.	6–10 exercises (including core and abdominal) with 8–15 repetitions performing 2–3 sets.	6–8 exercises (including core and abdominal) with 4–8 repetitions performing 2–3 sets.	1 or 2 power lifting exercises of 1–6 repetitions performing 3–5 sets. 4 or 5 other exercises (including core and abdominal) with 4–8 repetitions performing 2–3 sets.

Table 5.3 Progressing strength and power training cont.

Intensity of training	Body weight or light weights to develop muscular endurance.	Moderate resistance using the principle of progressive overload.	High resistance with 4–8 repetitions using the principle of progressive overload for strength development. Power lifts should be of moderate resistance, higher repetitions (6) and follow the principle of progressive overload as appropriate.	High to maximal resistance dependent upon the different cycles of the training programme (1–6 repetitions).
Periodised year	The type of training will remain fairly constant but frequency should reflect playing demands and be reduced accordingly.	The intensity of training should increase to meet the new training aims. The training programme should begin to reflect this and follow the structure of the single periodisation more closely.	Programmed cycles (of approx. 6 weeks) of training to develop strength and power need to be structured into the playing year.	Training should be highly structured following the principles of periodisation in order to obtain maximum gains.
	Training should take into account the stage of the playing year. As a rule, the amount of time dedicated to strength and power training is greatest in the off and pre-season, and the volume is reduced during the season due to playing commitments.			
LTAD	Training needs to take into account the demands of school, social and emotional needs as well as physical development. The aim is to develop sound technique and basic strength gains. Players whose physical development is in advance of their chronological age may progress to external resistance training if appropriate.	The physical development of younger players needs to be closely monitored to ensure they are ready for the increase in the intensity of weight training.	Players should have developed a sound strength base to allow them to begin power-based training. Technical competence should be high across a large number of lifts, as should their knowledge of training.	Players are now well-developed power athletes who possess a very high degree of technical skill and knowledge.

Progress to the next stage should only occur when the player is physically, technically and mentally ready. Players will not necessarily be ready to move on to the next stage just because they have spent a long time at the previous one!

Table 5.3 should provide you with a basic guide to the principles of programme design and progression. However, all training plans need to be individually tailored and designed by a qualified trainer.

Summary

Improvements in strength and power will have major benefits in terms of speed, jumping, winning collisions and the general physicality required for rugby. If correctly implemented, strength and power training will also have a positive influence on injury prevention.

Safety is the key when performing strength training; provided that the basic guidelines are followed with a gradual and appropriate progression, all players can undertake this form of training. Significant improvements in strength and power will not occur overnight and a structured and long-term programme is required to produce lasting results.

CHAPTER 6

Stretching and flexibility

Flexibility is the component of fitness that probably receives the least amount of attention from coaches and rugby players. It is often difficult for players to appreciate the improvements that this training brings. Flexibility assists general performance in rugby rather than having an area where it is obviously essential for performance on the rugby field. Given the choice, players would rather lift weights or do speed work as they understand where this fits into the game more clearly.

Improving flexibility and carrying out stretching is also associated with being injured, as these are activities generally prescribed by the physiotherapist. There is a responsibility on the coach to explain the role flexibility plays in speed, power and technical development so players are aware of the value and necessity of this training. As a result, it is of little surprise that the flexibility of players is generally poor, which has serious implications on a player's physical and technical development. In this chapter we will examine the different types of stretches and how they can be used in a player's training programme.

Flexibility needs to be trained and developed, as does any other component of fitness, and time needs to be specifically allocated to working on this area. The types of stretches carried out while warming up and cooling down are designed to prepare or assist the body in recovering from exercise, and although they will bring about improvements in flexibility they should not be seen as sufficient training in this area. Players need a structured flexibility programme to enable them to develop their general flexibility, while targeting any specific weaknesses that have been identified through medical assessment.

The benefits of flexibility

- The muscles and tendons are able to contract over a greater length, which increases the opportunity to produce power.
- Reduces the risk of injury as joints are able to move under control through a greater range of motion. Thus the body can perform more movements without the risk of a strain or sprain.
- Can help to break down scar tissue and decrease the likelihood of muscle strains.
- Enhanced flexibility improves localised and whole-body movements, promoting greater co-ordination of the body.
- Improves the execution of technical skills and increases the number of positions in which the body can successfully perform them.
- Can help to reduce the onset of fatigue as the contracting muscles work more effectively, thus conserving energy.
- Delays the loss of range of motion caused by ageing.

Movement, and thus athletic performance, depends on the efficiency of the muscular system. Muscular efficiency is optimal when the appropriate range of motion is available.

How does stretching improve flexibility?

Stretching lengthens muscle fibres and the connective tissue, which realigns muscle fibres in the direction of the tension, thus helping to repair scar tissue and restore it to its correct length and function. When you stretch a muscle not all of the muscle fibres are recruited – the more you stretch, the more fibres become involved and the greater the length of the stretch.

When you stretch (lengthen) a muscle a reaction called the 'stretch reflex' occurs, which attempts to resist the change in muscle length by contracting the muscle. This is the body's attempt to prevent injury by not allowing the muscle to become overextended. The more suddenly the muscle is lengthened, the more powerful this contraction will be; this is the basic principle behind plyometric training.

When the tension in the lengthened muscle exceeds a certain threshold a message is passed which overrides the message to contract. This allows the muscle to relax and is why stretches need to be held in order to reduce the effect of stretch reflex. Over time the muscle becomes more accustomed to the new length and it reduces the signal to contract, allowing further lengthening and improvements in muscle flexibility. It is easier to stretch a muscle when it is not trying to contract, which is why stretches need to be practised often and held for between 15 and 30 seconds for flexibility gains.

Types of flexibility training

The flexibility required by a rugby player is a combination of joint mobility, strength, co-ordination and specific proprioception. Players are actually subjected to different types of flexibility. When a player is moving this is referred to as 'dynamic', and when stationary it is known as 'static' flexibility.

Stretching is the performance of exercises to improve and maintain flexibility. There are various stretching methods used during training.

Dynamic – dynamic stretching sees the controlled movement of body parts with increases in stretch and speed. It involves the controlled swinging and rotation of the limbs and body parts through their normal range of motion.

Ballistic – ballistic stretching sees the moving body part go beyond its normal range of motion through a repeated bouncing motion. This form of stretching can be dangerous and is not recommended.

Static – the muscle is moved gradually into the stretched position and is held there. This type of stretching avoids any vigorous movement and as such bypasses the stretch reflex, resulting in the muscle being stretched in a relaxed state. This is the most commonly used stretching technique.

Passive – passive stretching is also known as relaxed stretching. A relaxed technique sees active stretching aided by a body part or partner. A partner is used to apply additional pressure to the area being stretched to increase the length of the stretch and the muscle fibres recruited

Active – this type of stretching sees a stretch with no assistance from any external forces.

Proprioceptive Neuromuscular Facilitation (PNF) – PNF uses relaxed passive stretching, followed by isometric contractions against a resistance, and then passive stretching again. PNF results in an increase in motion range. A muscle is taken into the stretched position and is then contracted against a fixed resistance, usually supplied by a partner. After this tension is held (for 2–15 seconds) the range of motion can be increased, thereby increasing the muscle fibres recruited. The resistance process should be repeated three or four times. These stretches should be carried out by a suitably qualified physiotherapist or trainer and is not recommended for young players whose bodies are still developing.

Timing of flexibility training and activity is essential in both development and recovery, but also in injury prevention. By neglecting flexibility and stretching the risk of injury increases, which in turn can lead to a decrease in performance in training and games. Stretching and specific flexibility programmes should be encouraged throughout the pre-season, the playing season and the close season. Specific sessions should be conducted weekly, with group stretching being conducted as part of warm-ups and cool-downs and within recovery sessions.

Flexibility and stretching are an essential component of fitness and when used efficiently can help to maximise both training and playing. If neglected, a player's potential may be compromised, which may in time lead to stiffness and a decrease in muscle range. Since players with a good level of flexibility are generally believed to be less susceptible to injury, with a planned and specific programme the risk of injury can be reduced. Without flexibility being improved after injury, players will very often suffer a relapse or new injuries as a result of this weakness when they resume training.

All stretching should take place when the body is warm as the soft tissues (muscles, tendons, skin and joint capsule) are easier to stretch and manipulate.

Stretches for flexibility

Prior to stretching a general warm-up should be carried out in which the core temperature is raised and the body prepared for the activity that is going to be undertaken.

The following is a programme of stretches that can be carried out to develop improved flexibility. Specific flexibility training needs to take place at least twice a week for any significant improvements to occur, at the same time observing the appropriate flexibility protocols while warming up and cooling down.

These stretches should not be painful as it takes time to develop improved flexibility. Stretches should therefore be controlled and performed at a moderate intensity so as not to cause damage to the muscle fibres.

Stretches should be held for between 15 and 30 seconds, with two or three repetitions for each stretch.

Calf stretch

Place your feet a stride's length apart with the right leg in front, leg slightly bent and face forwards, keeping the hips square and the chest high. Keep the heel of your left leg on the floor and the stretch will be felt down the calf of this leg. Hold and repeat for the opposite leg.

This stretch is often performed with the hands pushing against a wall to increase the intensity of the stretch. By bending the rear leg the stretch can be moved more to the Achilles tendon.

Hamstring stretch

Lying with your back flat on the floor and keeping the hips square, raise the right leg up towards your face with a slight bend at the knee. Ensure the hips and shoulders remain on the floor and the stretch will be felt in the hamstring of the right leg. Hold and repeat for the opposite leg.

You can assist the stretch by holding the raised leg between the knee and calf, ensuring that the hips remain on the floor. The raised leg can also be positioned on a wall, doorway or box for a similar effect.

Quadriceps stretch

Lie down on your left side with the hips square and your legs resting on top of each other, supporting your head with your left hand. Bend the knee of your top (right) leg, hold the foot and slowly pull it towards your buttock. Keep your knee in line with your hip and you will feel the stretch down the quadriceps of the right leg. Hold and then repeat for the opposite side.

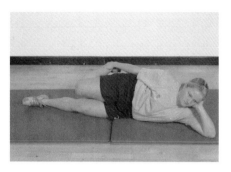

Hip and quadriceps stretch

Kneel down on one knee with the right leg bent at 90 degrees out in front. Keep the hips square and the back flat with the chest high. You will feel the stretch in the hip and quadriceps of the rear leg. Hold and repeat for the opposite leg.

Groin stretch

Lie on your back with the soles of your feet together and slowly lower the knees out and down. The stretch will be felt in the groin area of both legs.

This can be progressed into a sitting position with the hands holding the toes to increase the stretch.

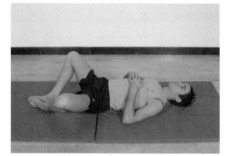

Gluteal stretch

Sit on the floor with the right leg flat and the left knee bent and crossed over by the right knee. Use your hands to pull the left knee up towards the right shoulder and you will feel the stretch in the left gluteal.

Back and gluteal stretch

Lie flat on your back and bring your left leg up towards your chest so that your foot is just above the knee of the right leg. With your right arm, move your left leg across and over the right leg. Keep your shoulders on the floor and you will feel the stretch in the back and gluteal; hold and then repeat for the right leg.

Middle back stretch

Sit on the floor with the left leg flat and the right leg bent and crossed over the left leg, level with the knee. Keep your upper body upright, put your left elbow into the outside of your right leg and turn your upper body to your right. Use your right hand to support your body as you hold the stretch; return to the middle and repeat for the opposite side.

Upper back stretch

Stand with your feet shoulder width apart with your knees slightly bent. Extend your arms out in front of your chest and link your fingers so that the palms of your hands face towards you. Push away from your chest, allowing your upper back to relax.

Chest and shoulder stretch

Stand in a doorway (or use a partner) with your feet shoulder width apart and your knees slightly bent. Extend your left arm out to the side so your hand can hold the door frame; turn your upper body to the right to feel the stretch in the chest and shoulders. Hold and repeat for the opposite side.

Shoulder stretch

Stand with your feet shoulder width apart with your knees slightly bent. Bring your left hand over your right shoulder and place your right hand on your left elbow. Hold this position and the stretch will be felt on the outside of the left shoulder. Repeat for the opposite shoulder.

Tricep and shoulder stretch

Stand with your feet shoulder width apart with your knees slightly bent. Bring both hands over your shoulders and slide your palms down your back, or work each arm independently, as in the photograph.

This is a selection of stretches that can be performed to improve general flexibility. Remember that a player could be highly flexible around the hip joint but have poor flexibility at other joints, therefore programmes should ideally be tailored to the individual's needs, having had their flexibility assessed by the club physiotherapist.

Stretches for warming up

The stretches described above are designed to improve flexibility and are not best suited for the purpose of preparing a player for playing. Dynamic stretches mimic the actions that a player will be required to perform in a game more closely and as such are a more suitable warm-up activity than static stretching.

These stretches can be performed individually, in small groups or as a whole team. They are often carried out in a line to replicate the defensive cohesion needed in rugby and to provide a means of mental preparation as well. Perform them over 10–15 m with a jog forwards, backwards or walk recovery between sets (2–4 sets of each stretch are recommended).

Pulse-raising exercises, including multi-directional running, skipping and ball handling, should be used to raise core body temperature before carrying out the dynamic stretches. It is also worth switching between stretching and ball handling to help maintain the mental focus of the players.

Examples of dynamic stretching

Due to the dynamic nature of the stretches, although specific muscle groups are targeted by the action, multi-joint mobilisation occurs in the majority of the exercises. Hence a number of muscles are activated during these activities, which also helps to develop body control and co-ordination. Good running technique (see pages 60–63) should also be reinforced during these exercises when possible.

These low-level dynamic stretches should be carried out before moving on to swings and rotational stretches.

Heel flicks

These target the hamstrings; flicking the foot to the groin or out to the side of the hips works the different muscles in this group.

High knees

Run and raise the knees up to hip height to stretch the hips and gluteals.

Ankle flicks

Walk, extend the leg and pull the toes up towards the face to stretch the ankle and calf.

Knee out/across skips

Push each leg up and out to the side in turn to stretch the hip and groin; perform the action across the body to target the hip specifically.

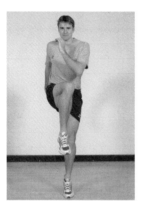 

These exercises can be progressed so that the height to which the knee is lifted is increased to extend the range of motion worked. All of these can be performed while moving backwards.

Walking calf stretch

Hold the stretch for a couple of seconds and then walk forwards to stretch the opposite leg.

Walking hamstring stretch

Hold the stretch for a couple of seconds, bring the toes up off the floor and then walk forwards to stretch the opposite leg.

Knee to chest walk (hips and gluteals)

Walk out and lift one knee to the chest, pulling it up with your hands on the shin. Hold for a couple of seconds, walk forward and perform the same exercise with the opposite leg.

Players should now perform some lateral running, gentle side-stepping and swerve runs. Some low-intensity striding can also be included.

Squats

These are a good lower body warm-up exercise that can again be performed multi-directionally.

Lunge walk

Lunge and walk forwards, backwards and to the side to work the lower limbs and joints. Inexperienced athletes should start with forward lunges and build up the number they perform in a warm-up gradually, before progressing to multi-directional lunges.

Players can now move on to performing swinging and rotational exercises. These should be performed in sets of 6–8 repetitions.

Swinging and rotational exercises

Over the gate

This assists hip rotation and mobilisation and can be performed with the rotation starting first from the inside and then from the outside.

Hamstring Russian walk

Walk out and raise the right knee to the chest, extend the leg keeping the toes to the sky and scrape the foot back to the floor.

Forward leg swings (use a partner or wall to perform)

These work the hip and hamstring in an increased range of motion; the standing heel should be raised off the floor to increase the range worked.

Lateral swings (use a partner or wall to perform)

Working the groin and hip region, again ensure the heel is off the floor. This exercise can also be performed lying on the ground.

Hip thrusts (use a partner or wall to perform)

Stand with the knees bent, hip width apart, with your hands on your partner's shoulders. This is a very dynamic exercise where the foot is driven from the floor so the knee is at hip height. The foot returns to a position on the floor slightly behind the body and is immediately driven back up again.

Lawnmower pulls

Kneel on all fours and lift your feet off the floor. Reach your right arm under your chest and through to the left side, then pull back so the arm comes out to the right.

Players should now perform some more striding and handling activities as well as some contact work to prepare them for the collisions they will make in the game.

This is only a selection of the stretches that can be performed and it is recommended that you attend an appropriate training course to further your understanding of these principles. More information on dynamic stretching, training courses and how it can be used in rugby can be found at www.saqinternational.com.

Stretches for cooling down

When cooling down a series of light dynamic stretches followed by some static stretches to restore tissue length should be undertaken, following the same principles as described above.

Flexibility and LTAD

FUNdamental (6–8 years) and learning to train (9–11 years)

General sports activities should be encouraged at this age. Participating in karate or gymnastics will help to develop flexibility, balance and co-ordination. Bending, twisting and stretching will form part of a multi-sports approach and should be sufficient at this age in terms of flexibility.

Training to train (12–14 years)

Players should undertake the appropriate pre- and post-activity stretching as well as working on flexibility in its own right. PNF stretching should be avoided due to the continued growth and development that players of this age are experiencing.

Training to compete (15–17 years), learning to win and training to win (18 years+)

Players should be including regular flexibility training as part of their training programmes to prevent injury and to aid the development of strength and power.

Summary

Warming up and cooling down effectively does not constitute training for this important component of physical fitness. Any physiotherapist will tell you that rugby players have notoriously poor flexibility and do little work to develop this area. They will also tell you that once a player has been cleared to play following an injury, they cease to continue with preventative flexibility, proprioception and muscle imbalance rectification, and invariably end up back in the physio room as a result.

Flexibility training needs to be encouraged primarily because of its importance for athletic development, and second as a means of injury prevention. This will help to change players' perceptions of flexibility training and its value to their training programmes, enabling them to understand the rugby benefits it can bring them.

CHAPTER 7

Core strength and stability

Core strength and stability is an area that has recently received an increasing amount of attention within the world of fitness and sport. Much of this has stemmed from the growth in the Pilates industry in the 1990s, which raised the profile of this type of training. Athletes and coaches have acknowledged the impact this area of the body has on all movement, and its importance in athletic performance.

The term 'core' refers to the foundation muscles of the abdominal and spinal region. Strong abdominal and spinal extensor muscles are essential in developing core strength (for movement) and stability. With weight training players tend to focus on the 'mirror muscles', the larger muscle groups in the body responsible for producing movement. As a result the muscles that stabilise the body to allow these muscles to function (the spinal and abdominal areas) are often neglected. This results in these larger muscles becoming dominant over the smaller stabilising muscles, which can have a negative effect on power and technique and lead to injury.

In order to develop strength and reduce the likelihood of injury, players need to develop their core before embarking on heavy strength or power training. If this area isn't trained, the body's capabilities of performing most physical tasks will be hampered.

The lower back and abdominal region is a major area of power production and links the upper and lower body. If you can harness and develop the link between the upper and lower body it stands to reason that you will be able to generate greater power in your movements. Without an efficient working core the power produced is limited or restricted.

To develop core stability players must learn and understand postural control before they can perform the exercises. By having the correct posture the contractions of the deep abdominal muscles can occur. Once posture is settled, a 'drawing-in' technique is used where the player pulls the belly button to the spine, which in turn tightens the gluteals. By performing this exercise, players will prevent stability and rotational problems. It is important that players have stability before they progress through the core exercises. Breathing is essential through each stage of a core exercise – by holding their breath players increase the stresses on the body and reduce the effectiveness of the exercise.

In order to develop the deep core muscles players should adhere to the following principles:

- **Concentration** – focusing on the movement and the specific muscles being worked enhances body awareness. Linking the brain and body also improves proprioception.
- **Centring** – focus on developing pelvic and scapula stabilisation by holding muscle contractions for at least 10 seconds.
- **Control** – movements should be controlled, maintaining stability and good posture. Technique should be pursued over intensity.
- **Core alignment** – working in a neutral position with joints held by the stabilising muscles encourages good posture and alignment.
- **Co-ordination** – use smooth movements as opposed to forcing out repetitions.
- **Breathing** – co-ordinate breathing control with abdominal work to help activate stabilising muscles and maintain focus on the exercise. Breathe in with the movement or action that initiates stability.

Super muscle?

It was generally believed that the rectus abdominis was the key muscle required to stabilise the core for movement, but it has since been shown that this is not the case.

The transversus abdominis is the first muscle recruited in any body or limb movement and plays a critical role in stabilisation of the body for movement. Training this muscle is therefore critical for stabilisation of the core area and thus the whole body.

Figure 6.1 Core muscles

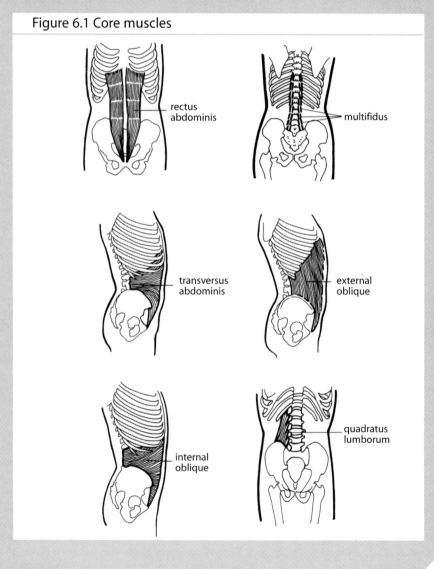

Core strength and stability in rugby

When you start to think about the movements and situations that players are subjected to during a game it becomes clear why developing core strength and stability is critical to the execution of skills and performance levels. Many of the positions a rugby players finds himself in result in the player being crouched down while leaning forward, as in rucking, lifting and tackling. This greatly increases the risk of a player developing lower-back problems, especially if the core muscles cannot provide the strength and stability to support this position.

The line-out

While in the air a jumper needs to rotate and reach in front, to the side or behind in order to reach the throw. Controlling these body movements is dependent upon the core muscles and their ability to hold the body in a stable position.

The scrum

When scrummaging it is critical for safety that the shoulders do not fall below the hips. If a player has a weak core or does not activate the core muscles, he will find it difficult to maintain a strong position. Without the core muscles activated the weight of the upper body will begin to head towards the ground, and any forces coming through the player from others in the scrum will only add to this.

Rucking and tackling

The basic position that we encourage players to take when preparing for any contact situation encourages the activation of the core muscles. Failure to do so reduces the power that can be generated in the contact situation and increases the likelihood of poor execution and injury.

As with scrummaging, without the core muscles activated the shoulders will slump and begin to point to the ground. This effectively separates the upper and lower body and will greatly reduce the force that can be generated in the contact. With the shoulders slumping forwards the power will also be heading down, making it easier for an opponent to push you to the floor as your power is already taking you there.

In contact situations core strength and stability are critical, and are also important when sprinting, changing direction, accelerating and decelerating.

Developing core strength and stability

Carrying out hundreds of sit-ups will not necessarily develop a strong core. Sit-ups work by flexing and extending the rectus abdominis muscles, but do not target the other core muscles, and therefore have a limited role in linking the upper and lower body for power production. Movements in rugby require much more rotation and stabilisation in the core area (passing, reaching to receive a pass, kicking) than they do flexion and extension. As such, these are the movements we should mimic in our training programmes.

As with all types of training there needs to be progression in the difficulty of the exercise, but not until the correct movement patterns and control of the targeted muscles have been achieved. This should be carried out on a stable surface (i.e. the ground) before incorporating the use of Swiss balls, wobble boards or jelly discs to increase the level of difficulty. When using weights for resistance always start light and then increase the weight. Most medicine ball work should start with a 1 or 2 kg ball to encourage the speed of movement.

Stabilisation exercises

Drawing in

Before attempting any of the more complex exercises designed to work the core muscles it essential that players are competent in performing the drawing-in action. Progressing before this has been achieved will result in poor technical execution of the exercises, resulting in the desired muscle groups not being trained and increasing the potential for injury while carrying out the exercises.

In order to begin to work the core muscles you need to recruit the transverse abdominis and multifidus muscles. Traditional sit-ups do not do this so players need to be taught how to target these muscles in order to develop their core stability.

Muscles targeted: transverse abdominis and multifidus.

1. Lie on your back with your knees bent, leaving a small gap between the floor and your lower back – this is the neutral lumbar position.
2. Relax all your stomach muscles and then draw in your lower abdomen – think about trying to pull your belly button towards your spine.
3. Hold this for 10 seconds then release and relax the muscles again for a few seconds before repeating the action.

Perform this 6 times.

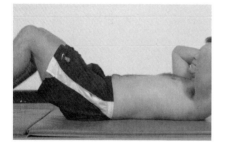 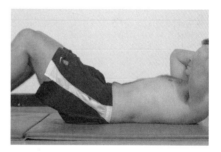

This will feel quite awkward at first and it will take some time before you can perform it without curling the abdominal muscles. Placing a kicking tee in line with the hips can help to focus the player on drawing this area down. Once you can successfully draw in while lying on your back, attempt it lying on your front, on all fours, sitting or kneeling with a ball held above your head.

Side raise

This is an excellent exercise that works a number of the core muscles and can be easily progressed once the player becomes competent with the technique.

Targeted muscles: obliques, erector spinae, abdominals, gluteals, latissimus dorsi and quadratus lumborum.

1. Lie on your side with your legs extended in a straight line.
2. Bend your lower arm to 90 degrees with your forearm on the floor directly under your shoulder.
3. Ensure your hips are directly in line, with one on top of the other.
4. Push your hips up until you are in a straight line; do not allow the hips to move forwards or backwards once you are in this raised position, but keep them balanced and do not rest on your shoulder.
5. Squeezing your gluteals and tensing the abdominals will help you to maintain your balance while holding this raised position.

Hold the position for 10 seconds when you first attempt this exercise and then return to the start position. Perform 6 times before changing sides. Eventually, you should aim to perform 2–3 sets of this exercise and gradually build up the hold times until you can maintain the position for 60 seconds.

Repetitions: 1 (30–60 sec)
Sets: 2–3
Rest time: 15–45

Progressions and variations: When in the raised position, lift the top leg so the feet are 6–12 inches apart; this increases the difficulty of the hold and activates the hip muscles. Instead of holding the position at the top, lower the hips so they are just above the ground then return to the top; repeat this for between 10 and 15 repetitions.

Superman

This exercise develops the muscles in the lower back and targets the muscles that provide rotational stability.

Targeted muscles: erector spinae, multifidus, transverse abdominis and obliques.

1. Kneel on all fours with your hands below your shoulders and knees below your hips.
2. Draw your abdominal muscles in while maintaining a neutral spine position, then slide one leg back and extend it out.

Hold the position for 10 seconds when you first attempt this exercise and then return to the start position. Perform 6 times before changing sides. Eventually, you should aim to perform 2–3 sets of this exercise and gradually build up the hold times until you can maintain the position for 60 seconds.

Repetitions: 1 (30–60 sec)
Sets: 2–3
Rest time: 15–45

Progressions and variations: Perform the exercise as described above, but when the leg is extended behind also raise the opposite arm out in front.

Push-up bridge

By using isometric (static) contraction, the deep abdominal muscles are again worked in this exercise to provide body stability. The push-up position requires the shoulder stabiliser muscles to perform a similar task, with the added benefit of the core and shoulder stabilisers working concurrently to stabilise the body.

Targeted muscles: erector spinae, multifidus, transverse abdominis and shoulder (scapular) stabilisers.

1. Assume the push-up position and draw in the deep abdominal muscles.
2. Hold this position for the desired time while maintaining good form at the head and lower back.

Repetitions: 1 (20–45 sec)
Sets: 2–3
Rest time: 20–45

Progressions and variations: Taking the arms out in front of the body increases the difficulty of this exercise. A Swiss ball/wobble board or other unstable surface can also be used to progress this exercise. Placing the feet as opposed to the hands on the Swiss ball puts greater demands on the shoulder stabilisers.

Back bridge

This exercise works the core abdominals as well as recruiting the upper leg muscles in order to create a stable work base.

Muscles targeted: erector spinae, multifidus, transverse abdominis, gluteals, hamstrings, iliotibial bands and quadriceps.

1. Lie with your shoulders on a Swiss ball with your hips and knees in line and your arms extended out to the sides.
2. Your feet should be flat on the floor with your knees bent at 90 degrees.
3. Place a rugby ball between your knees and squeeze while contracting the deep abdominal muscles.
4. Hold this position for the desired time.

Repetitions: 1 (20–45 sec)
Sets:　　　2–3
Rest time:　20–45

Back raise

This exercise predominantly targets the muscles of the lower back.

Targeted muscles: erector spinae, multifidus, transverse abdominis and obliques.

1. Lie face down on a Swiss ball with your feet on the floor, your knees bent and your hips on the top of the ball.
2. Place your hands by your head and bring your chest up off the ball until your back is straight – do not hyperextend the back.
3. Hold for a second and then return to the start position.

Tempo:　　　3–1–3
Repetitions: 10–15
Sets:　　　2–3
Rest time:　30–60

Progressions and variations: To increase the difficulty of the exercise, extend your arms out in front of your body.

Hanging leg raise

As well as working the core abdominal muscles, this exercise also recruits the hip flexor muscles to raise the legs.

Muscles targeted: erector spinae, multifidus, transverse abdominis, obliques and hip flexors.

1. Hang from a chin-up bar with your arms and legs fully extended horizontally.
2. A medicine ball/dumbbell is then placed between the feet and held in place by squeezing the legs together.

3. Contract the deep abdominal muscles, bend your knees and raise them towards your chest, flexing your toes and feet upwards throughout the action. Hold for one second.

4. Return to the start position by extending your legs back towards the ground.

Tempo: 3–1–3
Repetitions: 10–15
Sets: 2–3
Rest time: 30–60

Progressions and variations: As you bring your knees up towards your chest, rotate them out to the sides to target the oblique muscles.

Rotational exercises

In order to develop the core muscles in a manner that will be of most benefit to the rugby player, they need to be worked while rotating. This will progress from simple rotational stability and movement to highly explosive actions in which the positive transfer into rugby situations such as passing and tackling can easily be recognised.

Standing rotation

As well as working the core muscles, the transfer of this exercise into a passing action is obvious.

Muscles targeted: obliques, erector spinae, multifidus, transverse abdominis and shoulder (scapular) stabilisers.

1. Stand with your feet shoulder width apart, knees slightly bent and a handled weight or medicine ball directly in front of you at shoulder height, with the arms extended.
2. Contract the deep abdominal muscles and rotate your body to the left; your right heel will come off the floor as you rotate.
3. Rotate until the weight is in line with your shoulder, hold for one second and then rotate to return to the start position.
4. Repeat this action to your left.

Tempo: 3–1–1
Repetitions: 10–15
Sets: 2–3
Rest time: 30–60

Progressions and variations: Start with the weight slightly below shoulder height but to the side of the body, so you are slightly rotated. Squat down and rotate around, rising up out of the squat position and finishing with the weight at shoulder height on the opposite side of your body.

Wood chop

This exercise works the core muscles and requires stabilisation of the knees, hips, ankles and shoulders, making it an excellent whole-body stabilisation exercise.

Muscles targeted: obliques, erector spinae, multifidus and transverse abdominis.

1. Assume a squat position with a handled weight plate or medicine ball outside your right knee with your arms fully extended.
2. Contract the deep abdominal muscles and lift the weight to head height to the left side of your body.

3. Pause for a second, return the weight to the start position and repeat for the desired number of repetitions.
4. Rest and then perform the exercise for the opposite side.

Tempo: 3–1–1
Repetitions: 10–15 (each side)
Sets: 2–3
Rest time: 30–60

Progressions and variations: Perform this as a reverse wood chop, starting at the top and lowering the weight slowly, then raising it with a more explosive action. Carry out the exercise on one leg to increase the need for stabilisation, or use an unstable surface such as a wobble board.

Diagonal raise

This is very similar to the wood chop but the movement is performed closer to the body with greater rotation and allows for multi-joint activity, ending with the body fully extended. This is an excellent exercise for line-out lifters and jumpers.

Muscles targeted: obliques, erector spinae, multifidus and transverse abdominis.

1. Start in a squat position with a handled weight plate or medicine ball outside the left leg with the elbows bent.
2. Bring the weight up and across the body, rotating the hip to do so, and push up from the left foot.
3. Finish with the weight above the body on the right side, with your head looking up at it. Hold for one second.

4. Reverse the action to return to the start position.
5. Complete the desired number of repetitions, rest, then perform for the opposite side.

Tempo: 3–1–1
Repetitions: 10–15 (each side)
Sets: 2–3
Rest time: 30–60

Progressions and variations: Begin with 5 kg and increase the weight as required.

Dynamic rotational exercises

The following exercises are much more explosive than those that have been discussed previously. As a result they incorporate the fundamental principles of stability and rotation, but also bring in the additional component of power due to the dynamic nature of the exercise.

The use of medicine balls provides an excellent tool for developing this area. Players enjoy being challenged with new ideas and training practices that allow movements in rugby to be mimicked more closely than with the use of weights to provide resistance. The key to any form of power training is to concentrate on correct technical execution of the exercise, so begin with a light weight to develop technical competence.

There are a number of general throws that can be performed with a medicine ball against a wall to develop rotational power. Players should stand about 2 m away from the wall and catch the ball as it returns to them; the need to use a light ball and a structurally strong wall are again stressed. 6–10 repetitions and 2–3 sets should be performed, with the emphasis on the quality and speed of the throw rather than quantity or the weight of the ball.

Rotate and throw

1. Face the wall with the ball on your left hip; your knees should be slightly bent and your torso slightly rotated.
2. Throw the ball at the wall from waist height and catch it on its return.
3. You can alternate between sides or throw from the same side and then swap around to work both sides evenly.

Progressions and variations: Perform the exercise side-on or with your back to the wall to alter the degree of rotation. You can also vary the height at which the ball is thrown to alter the forces in play, and progress to one-legged throws.

Diagonal throw

1. Face the wall with the ball level with the left shoulder and the torso slightly rotated.
2. Rotate forwards towards the wall and throw the ball with a chopping action down into the ground so it bounces up against the wall.
3 Repeat the desired number of repetitions for each side.

Paired pass

As well as working the core muscles, the progression of this exercise into a passing action will be clear.

1. Stand with your feet shoulder width apart, knees slightly bent and a medicine ball directly in front of you at shoulder height, with your arms bent and elbows high as if you were passing a rugby ball.
2. Contract the deep abdominal muscles and pass the ball to your partner, who should be standing an appropriate distance away dependent upon the weight of the ball being used.

3. The partner, having caught the ball, then passes it back following the same key rules for a lateral pass.
4. Complete the required number of repetitions and repeat from the opposite side.

Repetitions: 6–10 (per side)
Sets: 2–3
Rest time: 30–60

Progressions and variations: This activity can be performed while standing on a jelly disc or wobble board to create an unstable surface, or while sitting on a Swiss ball. Performing the activity while standing on one leg increases the need for stability, while also reflecting the fact that one leg is often off the ground when passing in a game. Have the players' stagger increased so that they have to replicate pulling the ball (pass) back to a deeper angle of attack.

Off the top

This exercise is of particular benefit to line-out jumpers in developing shoulder stability, flexibility and rotational strength.

1. The player kneels on an exercise mat facing you, prepared to catch the medicine ball above his head.
2. The ball is thrown above head height to the player, who catches the ball, immediately rotates with it still above his head and passes to the scrum half.
3. The throw to the player should be varied (in front, behind and to the side) to replicate the need to adjust body position to take a slightly wayward throw in a game. The scrum half should also change positions and his distance from the catcher to mimic the need for the ball off the top to be passed to different positions.
4. Ensure the practice takes place for both sides.

Repetitions: 10 (per side)
Sets: 2–3
Rest time: 30–60 seconds

Progressions and variations: This activity can be performed while standing/kneeling on a jelly disc or wobble board to create an unstable surface, or while kneeling on a Swiss ball. Performing the activity while standing on one leg also increases the need for stability. A player can jump to take the ball with lifters to add more realism.

When should you do core work?

Core exercise should not always be carried out at the end of a training session. This can lead to players believing it is unimportant and something of an afterthought, and is often missed out if time is short.

Avoid performing core training before exercises that require stability of the core during the movement, such as power lifts, squats and lunges – you do not want to fatigue the core and then carry out such exercises, as you increase the likelihood of injury.

Core training and LTAD

FUNdamental (6–8 years) and learning to train (9–11 years)

At this age children should be experiencing a variety of different sports and no specific core training needs to be undertaken. Activities such as judo and gymnastics, which teach the child to understand balance and how the body reacts to different forces and movements, will assist core development.

Training to train (12–14 years)

Body weight exercise can be used to develop core stability and strength during training sessions. The basic techniques and value of core stability can be introduced and related to rugby-specific situations.

Training to compete (15–17 years), learning to win and training to win (18 years+)

Players are now reaching full physical maturation so core training needs to form part of their rugby and athletic development.

Summary

A strong core area will not only bring about improvements in strength, technique and safety, it will also reduce the chances of injury and in particular lower-back problems. Traditional abdominal work (such as crunches for the rectus abdominis) should be carried out, but it is important to balance them with stabilisation and rotational work to properly develop this area for the demands of rugby.

CHAPTER 8

Mind games

As coaches we are often quick to point out that a certain player 'lacks confidence' or 'bottles it when the pressure is on'. This may well be true, but do you as a coach possess the skills and knowledge to help rectify these shortcomings? Mental strength is often cited as the hallmark of a good player. If we believe this, then just as we spend time working on physical preparation and technical ability, time should be set aside for developing the mental skills required for successful performance.

Characteristics of mentally strong athletes

- Consistent performance regardless of opposition and other variables.
- Confident and positive outlook regardless of situation.

- Sees situations as opportunities not threats.
- Uses setbacks as a reference point to improve from.
- Controls situations rather than letting situations exert control.

This chapter will examine some simple techniques that can be put into practice with individual players, and the team as a whole. It will enable you to identify players' mental strengths and weaknesses, and to devise coping strategies to bring out the best in them. Coaching should place players under stress in a controlled environment – gaining experience of such conditions and the emotions that they produce in practice increases the likelihood that they will cope successfully in a competitive situation. An example is given in the box below.

Simulation training

- When playing a team whose back row is very quick and puts pressure on the fly half, set up controlled practices to replicate this. Move the offside line a metre closer to the fly half so he can experience the stress of having less time. This will prepare him mentally for the pressures he will experience in the contest.
- In refereed training matches deliberately penalise one side harshly to see how they cope with poor decisions and the impact it has on their performance.
- Practice defending/attacking with 14 players to simulate a player having been sin-binned; this will help the team to prepare for such occasions.

It is worth reiterating that players are individuals and as such will have different psychological strengths and weaknesses that need to be identified and catered for. This is not always easy. Psychological weaknesses are often hidden by the player, or the player may be genuinely unaware that certain behaviour is counterproductive.

Confidence

This is quite often used to explain away all success and failure. In sport, confidence is essentially a feeling of having an expectation of succeeding. The most successful performers tend to have high aspirations and are more willing to 'try things'. They generally perceive challenging situations as opportunities rather than threats; as such they have a high desire to succeed and a low fear of failure.

Being extremely confident is not necessarily a guarantee of success, but in situations where teams are evenly matched this can often make the difference. The more successful players are, the more confident they become. Confidence is a mental state, a feeling and perception that a player has about themselves; as such this view can be altered or developed through mental training.

Developing confidence

Past experience

Focusing on past success in training and matches is a key way of building confidence. It is important that players leave sessions in a positive frame of mind, knowing when they have been successful. Videoing training sessions and matches is highly effective in this regard as players can 'see' themselves performing. It also provides a visual reference that can be used for mental imagery.

Vicarious experience

Confidence can be improved by seeing other players performing a task successfully. This is most relevant when the player observed is of a similar level, as they can relate to this performance; it is the 'if they can then I can' syndrome. A good example of this is the four-minute mile – a number of athletes were within a second of this for a decade before Sir Roger Bannister broke the mythical barrier. Once he went under four minutes he opened the floodgates and within 18 months 16 athletes had followed his lead.

Verbal persuasion

As a coach you are in a position to instil confidence in your players by telling them they have the skill and ability to perform certain tasks. What you tell a player needs to be credible and quantifiable; telling them they have the ability to win the game may be correct, but it is very imprecise. By making statements specific you will provide a more useable cue for players to relate to during a match. This could be a quiet word to your winger telling him he has the speed to take his man on the outside, or vociferously congratulating your front row at half-time in front of the rest of the team for the way they have dominated the scrums.

Stress/anxiety and arousal

The physical nature of rugby and the diversity of technical skills and tactical situations mean players are subjected to the full spectrum of human emotions during a match. Controlling these emotions is very often the critical factor in determining successful performance.

Stress and anxiety present themselves in the following forms:

- feeling of apprehension
- physical tension
- fear of what might happen
- a personality trait or a temporary state caused by situational pressures.

Anxiety has a negative effect on performance; it decreases the ability to identify relevant and irrelevant information and makes it more difficult to select appropriate responses. Those who suffer from severe anxiety will often waste time carrying out irrelevant tasks that can cause attention levels to drop, and performance to deteriorate accordingly.

Trait anxiety

Our natural reaction to situations; you are more likely to see situations as threatening if you have high trait-anxiety levels.

Players with a low level of trait anxiety will generally be fairly laid back and cope well with stress, whereas those with high trait anxiety are more likely to be adversely affected by stress. The latter tend to feel uncomfortable in tense situations such as trials and big matches; relaxation techniques and triggers may help to reduce these feelings of stress.

State anxiety

A temporary condition in sport due to high levels of arousal because of a specific situation. This could be an important kick, throw, match, or playing in front of a big crowd including family and friends.

Controlling anxiety and arousal

Just because a person gets anxious and nervous it does not mean they can't be a successful rugby player. Discussing and reinforcing the fact that nerves can be coped with will be beneficial to all players. Nerves are only a problem if the player does not have a strategy to cope with them.

As already stated, being overly anxious can also result in underperformance. This can lead to players 'hiding', not wanting to get involved in the game through a fear of making mistakes. They can become so stressed that they can't perform basic skills. The stress and pressure of certain situations can result in simple tasks being performed poorly: for instance, Gavin Hastings missing a kick in front of the posts in the 1991 World Cup semi-final. Being over-excited (over-aroused) can have a negative effect on performance in other ways – players can be so 'up for' a game that they lose focus and control.

Players can also suffer from under-arousal, which can also have a negative effect on performance. This can often occur when playing opponents who are perceived to be of little threat, or if a match has no significance, or in the second half of a game in which you have already scored a lot of points and put the result beyond doubt.

Being too anxious, or under- or over-aroused, affects the ability to maintain focus on the things that are important to successful performance. Players need to find a balance in their arousal levels that enables them to perform without being overly anxious or aroused – an 'optimal arousal level'. A good example of a team and individuals being in an optimal state of arousal would be the England players in the 2003 Test match at Twickenham against South Africa. Here, despite attempts to distract them through physical intimidation and provocation, they remained focused on the relevant information required to perform, and ignored the irrelevant. Rugby is such a multi-skilled sport that arousal levels need to be controlled, lowered or raised depending on the skill to be performed and the situation it is being performed in.

All players need to ensure that they control their anxiety levels in order to ensure optimum performance, which means looking after the mind through mental imagery and looking after the body with relaxation techniques. This should take place as part of the normal training week, as well as in the immediate build-up to, and during, a game.

How much relaxation, mental imagery and 'psyching up' are required to establish the desired arousal level for the game differs for each individual. Players need to develop their own routine that enables them to perform to their true capability without being negatively influenced by anxiety or arousal.

All players will have been stressed, over-aroused and under-aroused at some point before and during matches. They need to be able to recognise these feelings and have the tools (see coping strategies on pages 170–77) in their locker to deal with these situations when they arise.

Optimal arousal

We often hear it said that players are in the 'zone'. This refers to the zone of optimal functioning, a narrow band of arousal level that facilitates the best performance in a particular activity. The zone differs for different skills, activities, situations and individuals. For example, the zone required for throwing in at a line-out (a 'fine' skill) will require a different level of arousal than performing a tackle (a 'gross' skill), due to the nature of the movements and mental concentration levels. Gross skills involving dynamic movement of the whole body or limbs generally require a higher level of arousal. More technical, fine skills often benefit from a lower level of arousal for successful performance, as being over-aroused makes controlling these delicate movement patterns more difficult.

Performance profile

In order to improve performance it makes sense to evaluate present skill levels first and set targets in terms of the performance that is desired. A useful tool to accomplish this is the performance profile. The profile is a questionnaire that looks at the physical, technical, tactical and psychological components of rugby. It encourages self-reflection and analysis by players, promoting a better understanding of what they need to do to improve. It will also enhance a player's understanding of the skill requirements for their position, and the game in general.

The profile builds up a picture of the individual's strengths and weaknesses from which training programmes can be planned and adapted, and long- and short-term goals for improvement set. The player is pivotal to this and is actively involved in the setting of goals and the decision-making process. By empowering players in this way they are more likely to be motivated to achieve the agreed goals.

Stage 1 – Introducing the theory

The concept should be explained to the player, why it is being done and the benefits this will have to their game. There are no right or wrong answers, only personal evaluations.

Stage 2 – Designing the profile

The design of the profile should again be player-led. Get the players to work in groups to build up the 'design' of the profile. This can be done by asking the players to list the qualities that an elite rugby player possesses. You can prompt the players if required by using the following headings:

- Physical
- Core Skills
- Psychological
- Professional
- Technical
- Tactical.

This provides the coach with an insight into the players' perceptions of the skills and abilities required for successful performance.

Stage 3 – Profiling

Once you have the design of the profile from the players, they then need to complete it. Players fill in the profile and give themselves a score for how they view their competence in these areas, and how important they perceive this aspect of play is to their position. They then subtract their current score from the ideal standard, which produces a discrepancy mark. The higher the discrepancy mark, the greater the need for intervention through physical, technical, tactical or psychological training, diet or education. This should lead to an improvement in player performance and a reduction in the discrepancy score over time. It also provides players with a detailed self-analysis and the coach with a clear insight into how the players view their own strengths and weaknesses.

The aim of the profile is to monitor the perceived success of any intervention and training strategies that have been implemented. Regular updating of the profile can also have a positive effect on player motivation, as they see their marks changing and moving closer towards their ideal standard.

Coaches should also fill in the questionnaire and compare it with the player's score, thus highlighting any major differences in how the player and coach perceive performance.

The table below provides an example of the psychological section of the profile for a fly half.

Table 8.1 Sample psychological profile

Psychological	Importance for position (IP)	Ideal standard (IS)	Current standard (CS)	IS–CS discrepancy
Performing under pressure	10	10	8	2
Consistency	9	10	8	2
Confidence	9	10	6	4
Concentration	9	10	5	5
Refocusing after errors	9	10	5	5

In this case it would appear that maintaining concentration and refocusing after errors are the priority areas for improvement. Mental rehearsal techniques could be used to address the concentration issue, while self-talk and triggers would help the performer refocus after making an error.

The information from the profile should be used by the coach and player to set agreed goals and training strategies to improve technical, tactical, physical and mental performance.

Benefits

- Highlights perceived strengths and weaknesses.
- Helps to monitor progress.
- Provides a comparison of athlete's and coach's vision of requirements for successful performance.
- Pinpoints differences and agreement on assessment of performance standard.
- Promotes discussion between player and coach.

These are the major strengths of the profile; its player-centred approach involves the performer at all stages and can be a major tool for the coach in helping to improve performance.

Goal setting

The performance profile is in many ways an audit, providing coaches and players with a starting point from which to work. Once we know where we are in terms of which skills/attributes are most important and need developing, it is then logical to decide what we want to do by setting goals. It is worth writing down your overall rugby goals for six months, a year and two years' time – these will be your long-term goals and the overall aim towards which you are working. Once these reference points have been agreed the training programmes and areas to be worked on can be devised.

There are many different types of goals – they can be long term, short term, outcome (result) orientated or performance orientated. Goals can relate to physical, technical, tactical and mental development. All are relevant and need to be included in the training and playing programmes of your athletes. Whichever type of goal you are working towards, you need to follow the same basic laws.

Positive language

Use positive as opposed to negative terminology in your goals. 'I will stay calm and focused on my game, ignoring the comments from the touchline,' instead of 'I won't be wound up by the crowd.' 'I will' rather than 'I won't' or 'will not'.

All goals should be SMARTER:

Specific –   Write down exactly what you want to achieve. It should be performance related and relevant to the skill you are trying to develop.

Measurable –   You need to be able to assess if the goal has been achieved. Try to make the goal measurable by providing a quantifiable target.

Agreed –   Players should set and agree the goals with their coach as part of the decision-making process.

Realistic –   Goals that are unobtainable will decrease motivation, as will goals that are too easily achieved.

Timed –   Set a timescale in which the goal will be achieved; this helps to focus the player on the task.

Evaluated – Progress towards the goal needs to be reviewed at regular intervals to assess progress.

Recorded – Writing down and recording the goal helps to reinforce the task
at hand and provides a visual reference point.

Short- and long-term goals

In order to achieve long-term goals we need to be continually setting and
working towards short-term goals. Having a long-term aim can appear rather
distant and daunting – players can easily be overawed by this and lose confidence and motivation. It is therefore advisable to break this goal down into
more achievable short-term goals that act as rungs on a ladder to achieving the
overall goal.

Figure 8.1 Example of a goal-setting ladder for punt accuracy

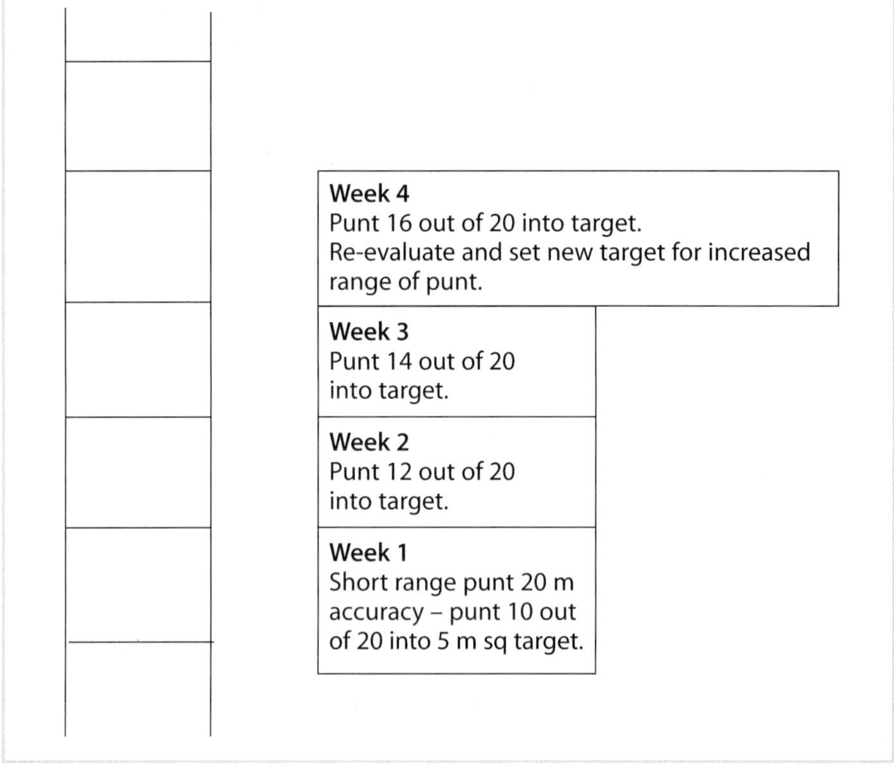

Week 4
Punt 16 out of 20 into target.
Re-evaluate and set new target for increased
range of punt.

Week 3
Punt 14 out of 20
into target.

Week 2
Punt 12 out of 20
into target.

Week 1
Short range punt 20 m
accuracy – punt 10 out
of 20 into 5 m sq target.

Outcome goals and performance goals

Outcome goals

As the name suggests, these are to do with the end result, such as winning a match or making a team. There is nothing wrong with having such goals as we all want tangible success as a reward for our efforts. Such goals can also be a source of great motivation during a game or while training, although there are many variables influencing our ability to achieve these goals, some of them beyond our control, such as luck, a referee's decision or a coach's selection preference. As such, it is important that we do not place ultimate success purely on outcome-led goals, as achieving them may not be totally within our control.

Performance goals

If you set and achieve performance-based goals then you will be improving your performance and be more likely to achieve the outcome goal. This type of goal focuses on performing specified skills or tasks to a certain level, such as kicking accuracy or tackles made/missed. Performance goals are compared against your own previous levels of performance and thus are more realistic and measurable than outcome goals. They provide a much better indicator of improvement and the level of performance rather than relying on the outcome of a match as the measure of success.

Sample goal

'I want to improve the accuracy of my goal-kicking.'

Q. Does this goal statement meet the SMARTER acronym, use positive language and is it performance based?
A. No

A more effective goal would be:

'I will develop the accuracy of my goal-kicking by being able to kick eight out of ten on the 22-metre line and between the 15-metre lines within four weeks.'

Goals should be recorded and written down to provide a reference point for re-evaluation and to keep them prominent in the player's mind.

Table 8.2 Sample goal-setting record

Area of development	Achievement method	Target	Timing
1. Mental I will remain calm in pressure situations and make good decisions.	Practise relaxation techniques and triggers during practice and matches.	Record pressure situations and monitor decisions and performance level.	Re-evaluate in 4 weeks.
2. Technical I will increase range of motion of my arm drive when sprinting.	Visualisation and reaffirming core running principle drills. Perform specific arm technique work for 5 min each day.	Video comparison of before and after training to determine whether correct technique has been learned.	Re-evaluate in 6 weeks.
3. Physical I will improve my speed over 30 m – currently 4.6 sec.	Perform 1 extra speed or plyo-metrics session per week as devised by conditioning coach.	Reduce 30 m time to under 4.5 sec.	By the start of the pre-season.
Player: Signed:			
Coach: Signed:			
Date: Review date:			

Coping strategies

There are a number of strategies that can be used to help players to manage the pressures and stress they will encounter during a game of rugby. When introducing these techniques to your squad, you need to create a conducive environment where they will not be disturbed and where they can concentrate on the activity.

Mental imagery

This is a technique that involves the player imagining himself in a certain situation performing a specific skill or activity. The player should visualise himself performing the skill successfully, enjoying the activity and being satisfied with his performance.

Jonny Wilkinson's performances in the World Cup have highlighted the use of mental imagery as a tool to aid performance. The meticulous routine that he carried out before each kick at goal was part of a mental strategy to cut out crowd noise and other irrelevant stimuli so he could focus solely on the task of converting the try. Mental imagery can reduce feelings of stress and anxiety and help to bring the player to the optimum level of arousal.

Figure 8.2 What is Jonny doing?

The hands joined create a barrier against the outside world, cutting out noise and other distractions and providing a cocoon in which he can relax, slow down his breathing and concentrate on visualising the strike and contact with the ball.

He pictures an imaginary woman called Doris, who sits in a particular seat in the stand behind the goal, holding a can of Coke. As Wilkinson prepares to kick, he visualises the flight of the ball ending up in Doris's lap, knocking the drink out of her hands. 'The idea was that, instead of aiming at the posts, you were aiming at something specific 30 yards back,' he said. 'That way we changed the emphasis of where I was aiming and it made me really kick through the ball.'

Wilkinson 'hardens' his kicking foot by tapping his left toe on the grass before he kicks, usually in two sets of three taps, thus helping the foot to adopt the shape and the tension he wants when he hits the ball.

This kind of imagery often takes place immediately prior to performing a skill, and is particularly relevant to fine skills such as kicking and the line-out throw. It can also be used prior to the match to 'see' successful performance against the immediate opposition, as well as during the match to maintain focus on the skills to be performed. The positive effect this practice has on reaffirming correct techniques and developing self-confidence makes it an important method in developing mental strength and improving performance.

The visualisation process could last a few seconds or 15 minutes or so depending on the situation and aims of the session. It can be used individually or collectively, the pack using imagery to see themselves engaging at a scrum, the back three successfully working together to perform a counter attack, or the backs executing a strike move.

Why do it?

- **Motivation** – use images of successful performance against future opposition.
- **Success** – seeing yourself performing well can promote confidence and the belief that you can achieve your goals.
- **Skills** – helps to reinforce learning and the use of appropriate techniques by seeing yourself performing the skill.
- **Familiarisation** – visualising playing in a particular stadium against certain opposition or running a set move can help to reduce anxiety associated with playing certain teams, opponents or venues.
- **Preparation** – visualisation of the events to come with successful outcomes helps to establish positive pre-competition feelings and develop a positive focus.
- **Refocus** – if you are underperforming, visualisation can help to refocus you on the task at hand by providing an example of successful performance.

Practising skills with this technique can help to strengthen the link between the mind and muscles, making the performance of skills more automatic and learned.

How to do it?

Imagery is most effective when combined with physical practice; this is also useful for the coach as it will help to maintain the players' concentration levels during training and reaffirm the correct technique in their minds. Having physically cleared a ruck, for example, the player can then replay what he has just done through imagery – the kinaesthetics involved in the point of contact, the bend in the knees and the power as he stepped into his opponent and cleared them out. He can then use imagery to reinforce this learning – performing the task physically will make the imagined version much clearer and more realistic.

Kinaesthetics is the sense by which movement, weight and position of the body and its parts are perceived. It is heavily reliant on the sense organs, in particular proprioceptors in the muscles, tendons and joints. These tell the player about the state of muscle contractions and are critical for producing smooth and controlled movements.

Concentrate on:

- Relaxing and focusing on creating a perfect image of the skill you want to perform.
- Utilising your senses.
- Making the image in your head specific to the situation you are in: pitch, opposition, smells, weather and colours.
- Thinking about the techniques that make up the skill and then watching yourself performing the skill.
- Watching yourself performing the skill from different angles to obtain a clear image of what you want to achieve.

As with all techniques, this needs to be practised regularly and in different situations. Specific imagery sessions should be introduced into players' training programmes, or a pre-match imagery programme could be devised with players.

Familiarise yourself with the example below before carrying it out with your players.

- Sit the players down and get them to close their eyes.
- Encourage them to visualise a rugby pitch (ideally where they will play their next game).
- Then read out the example overleaf, slowly and clearly, emphasising as many senses as you can to help the players build up a detailed mental picture of the required technique.
- Once they can do this, ask them how they would feel now about taking a high kick.
- They should feel more confident and should now try the technique for themselves.

- Get them to spend a few minutes visualising two skills they feel are important to their position.
- Encourage them to think about the technique in as much detail as possible in their imagery.

Example:

Prior to a game a full back sits in the dressing room and visualises successfully catching a high ball.

'The wind is calm and the sun is on my back; as the line-out forms on the halfway line I talk to both my wingers and confirm with them that their start positions are fine with me.

'The ball is caught at the front of the line-out by the opposition lock, who drops it down to the scrum half who passes to the fly half. He kicks the ball high into the air. I judge from the flight and pace that the ball will come down 10 m inside the 22 m line and 15 m from touch.

'I start running towards the ball's landing area, see my wingers coming back to support me and call that I will take the catch. As the ball drops I drive up off my right leg and reach my hands up to pull the ball into my chest. As I am in the air I turn my body slightly to shield the ball from the opposition and bring my knees up to protect myself while I am in the air.

'I keep my eye on the ball, feel it come into my hands, cradle it into my chest and call for the mark. As I land I bend my knees to soften my landing, and push off as I land to avoid the oncoming defender.

'I hear the referee blow his whistle and call "Mark". I step back to the mark, take three slow breaths and start to visualise a long kick to touch.'

Relaxation

Relaxation is crucial to ensure that players are mentally and physically ready to perform. Physical relaxation reduces the tension in the muscles, allowing them to contract and extend to their full range. Mental relaxation reduces stress and anxiety, which helps to reduce negative thoughts and create the optimal state of arousal.

Relaxation

A controlled and stable state of arousal that is lower than the normal waking state.

A relaxation session could last for 30 minutes as part of your psychological training, a few minutes in the dressing room prior to kick-off or a few seconds during a game before you perform a skill.

Progressive muscle relaxation (PMR)

This technique works by tensing muscle groups from head to toe for a few seconds and then releasing them in sequence. This can be conducted in a group or individually to develop players' relaxation skills and to encourage them to make the most use of their time away from training.

Loosen up
- Loosen clothing and remove shoes.
- Lie on your back on a comfy surface with a pillow for your head and close your eyes.
- Let the body go limp with your shoulder blades flat against the floor.
- Roll your feet and shake your legs.
- Shake your arms and roll your hands against the floor.
- Slowly roll your head from side to side.

Legs
- Raise your left leg 6 inches off the floor and pull your toes towards the body; hold this position for a count of 10, then say 'release' to yourself, stop tensing and let your leg drop. Feel the tension leave your leg and it feels warm, heavy and loose – repeat these words to yourself and feel the weight, heat and relaxation in your leg.
- Repeat this procedure and then do the same for your right leg.

Perform a similar process for the other body parts by tensing and then relaxing the muscles. Players can make their own tapes describing the activity for each body part, although pre-recorded relaxation tapes are available on the Internet, from coaching bodies (such as Coachwise) and health shops.

Breathing easily

Being able to control your breathing is a simple way to relax the body and can easily be applied during a match to control stress and arousal levels. To introduce this technique to your players you again need an appropriate environment where they will not be disturbed and where they can concentrate on the activity.

Read the instructions slowly and clearly to aid players to fully understand the process.

- Lie down on your back.
- Inhale slowly and deeply through your nose for a count of four. Hold the breath for a count of four.
- This should be a comfortable pause, then exhale slowly through your mouth saying 'release' as you do so. Let out as much air as you can, feeling your chest and shoulders drop and the tension leave with your breath.
- Repeat this 10 times.
- Then inhale slowly and deeply through your nose for a count of four. Hold the breath for a second, let it go and say 'release' as you do.
- Repeat 10 times.
- During a game, if you feel tense recall the calm feeling you have now and perform a shortened version of this exercise. You will begin to feel the tension leaving and the calmness returning.

Self-talk and triggers

This is another strategy which can be introduced to your players' mental training programme in order to develop self-confidence and motivation, and encourage positive thinking. The theory is simple: if you are thinking positively and saying positive things to yourself you are more likely to perform well; the opposite is the case for negative talk.

In training or games players can lose concentration or become upset and distracted as they make mistakes. Self-talk should be used to ensure players' state of arousal is at the optimum level for performance.

Self-talk should be short and concise; the word you use should be a trigger that is a reference to a particular response or action. You can also use a physical action to break the negative thought pattern associated with a mistake. When a player says this word or performs this action (e.g. claps hands twice) it triggers a pre-learned response to calm down, put the error out of their mind and look forward to the next task they must perform.

The use of trigger cues, as well as being a coping strategy to reduce anxiety and stress, can also be used as a coaching aid. The use of a particular word could be associated with the correct way of performing a skill – for instance the word 'bullet' could be used by a winger to chase long kicks. When he says this word it triggers feelings of speed and he focuses on explosive leg drive, relaxed upper body and utilising his arms for propulsion.

An example of how this can be used to encourage learning could be for hitting rucks. Once you have demonstrated the correct technique, get the players to clear the ruck then, just before contact, they should say the trigger word to remind them of the correct form. This should be a strong word such as 'smash' or 'hit', which is more likely to stimulate the desired response and the aggressive contact that the skill requires.

As a coach you can also introduce trigger words that, when used, elicit a certain response in the players. The word 'bulldog' could be the trigger to prompt a highly aggressive defence when defending in your own 22, focusing on putting the ball carrier down behind the gain line. This needs to be practised and bought into by the players, who know the response that is required and the state of mind that goes with it.

Some players write trigger words on their wrist strapping to reinforce what they are trying to achieve and to help keep them in the optimal performance state.

Talk to your players about how they react when they make mistakes; explain that getting worked up can have a negative effect by increasing anxiety levels and making errors more likely.

Point out that a mistake cannot be undone and there is no point dwelling on it during the game. Highlight the importance of being able to put mistakes out of their minds and concentrate on what they can do next to make a contribution to the team.

Mind games and LTAD

FUNdamental (6–8 years) and learning to train (9–11 years)

At this age children require regular positive reinforcement to provide the motivation to continue playing. Simple tasks, skills and games should be used to ensure that all players have the opportunity to experience success. A basic understanding of the rules and acceptable levels of behaviour should be introduced.

Training to train (12–14 years)

Training can take on a more technical nature as players have an increased capacity to make decisions and execute tactical strategies. A basic introduction to psychological techniques should occur to help players cope with the increased number of stressful situations they will encounter during a game.

Training to compete (15–17 years), learning to win and training to win (18 years+)

Players can cope with multiple strategies, particularly towards the end of the 'training to compete' stage. They are developing the capacity to analyse their own performance and the full range of coping strategies; other psychological techniques can be introduced. The development of mental toughness and group dynamics should also be explored.

Summary

In this chapter we have explored a number of practical techniques that, as coaches, you will be able to implement with your players. The key to learning any new skill is to practice the technique; it is also important that you identify the goal and devise a strategy to achieve it. Evaluating progress towards these mental goals is vital for enhancing these skills and establishing what is working and what new strategies need to be introduced.

Developing your players' mental strengths will have benefits in terms of helping them deal with situations they will encounter on the pitch. Perhaps more importantly, though, it will also help to develop the skills and qualities required to fulfil their potential, helping them find the will to prepare to win.

CHAPTER 9

Nutrition: eating to play

This chapter will examine the need for a balanced diet in order to maintain a healthy lifestyle and to perform on the rugby pitch. What and when to eat, the use of sports drinks and how to gain and lose weight will all be covered, providing you with the basic knowledge to start making improvements in your players' diet. Players will commit to a structured training programme without too much persuasion, but will neglect to do the same with their diet. However, without the correct diet any gains from training will be minimised, so it is vital that coaches reinforce the basics of good nutrition with their players.

Food as fuel

The body requires fuel in order to function to its full potential, gaining this fuel from the quantity, quality and type of food eaten. This in turn determines the amount of fuel and how it is produced, and subsequently your levels of performance.

An athlete's diet serves two main purposes: first, to provide energy to train and perform; second, to promote growth, repair and recovery from this physical exertion. As not all foods provide us with the same amounts of energy, it is important to understand these differences in order to ensure nutritional intake is appropriate.

There are three major energy stores in the body, the largest of which is body fat (adipose tissue). The body also derives energy from carbohydrate, which is converted to glycogen and stored in the liver and muscles. Protein stored in the muscles can be used for energy production although it cannot be stored for later use like carbohydrate and fat.

Food is digested, absorbed and metabolised to release energy that the body can then use. Below is a breakdown of the amount of energy that one gram of these food sources provide.

Table 9.1 Energy from different food sources

Food source	Energy per gram
Carbohydrate	4 kcal
Fat	9 kcal
Protein	4 kcal
Alcohol	7 kcal

Measuring energy in food

Calories are used to define the amount of energy present in different food types. A calorie is the amount of heat (energy) required to increase the temperature of one gram of water by one degree centigrade. One kilocalorie (kcal) is equivalent to 1000 calories and is more commonly used on food labelling.

Fats provide more than twice the energy of carbohydrate or protein, although it is not the best source of energy for rugby players due to the way it is broken down to produce energy.

Carbohydrate

The preferred energy fuel for the muscles is glucose. Glucose is formed from the breakdown of carbohydrates (sugars and starches, e.g. bread, rice, pasta, potatoes, breakfast cereals) and is stored as glycogen in the muscles and liver. The body can only store a limited amount of glycogen and thus carbohydrate levels need to be regularly topped up to ensure this energy source is available.

As exercise intensity levels rise, the body gains more of its energy needs from glycogen stored in the muscles; although this produces less energy per gram than fat, it releases the energy more quickly, which meets the demands for higher intensity activity. Anaerobic activity relies almost solely on glycogen for its energy production, whereas the aerobic system uses a combination of fat and glycogen to meet energy needs.

In intermittent high-intensity exercise such as rugby, a heavy demand is placed on the body's glycogen stores. Depletion of these stores will lead to fatigue, poor energy levels and reduced ability to recover from training sessions. Carbohydrate is the most important source of energy to fuel the exercising muscles, the brain and central nervous system.

Fat

Fat is stored primarily in the organs and under the skin; how this fat is distributed around the body is dependent upon the genetic make-up of the individual. It is difficult to spot-reduce fat from specific areas of your body by exercise, but you can reduce the overall amount of fat your body stores.

Fat is utilised as an energy source primarily during low-intensity exercise and prolonged endurance exercise. Unlike carbohydrates, there is no risk of running out of fat as a fuel source in even the leanest of athletes. Fat produces large amounts of energy, but it does so slowly, which makes it an appropriate source of energy for low-intensity exercise.

Fat is a vital part of our diet, providing essential fatty acids and fat-soluble vitamins and minerals. Although a fat-free diet should never be attempted, too much fat in the diet may lead to obesity and its associated health risks, including heart disease.

Fat in food is composed of two main types of fatty acids, saturated and unsaturated (polyunsaturated or monounsaturated). The fat in food is a combination of all of these fats, although the proportion of each varies greatly from food to food.

Unsaturated fats

Polyunsaturated fatty acids (PUFA)

These are an essential part of the diet and play an important role in reducing blood cholesterol levels. There are two types of polyunsaturates: those from the seeds of plants such as sunflower oil and soya oil (Omega 6), or those mainly from fish oil (Omega 3). There is good evidence that eating oily fish (salmon, mackerel and so on) helps reduce the risk of heart disease – for this reason alone it should be included in your diet at least once a week.

Monounsaturated fatty acids (MUFA)

These have been found to help lower the amount of LDL cholesterol in the blood (the type of cholesterol known to increase the risk of heart disease) without lowering HDL cholesterol (known to have a protective effect against heart disease). Monounsaturates can be incorporated into your diet through olive oil, rapeseed oils, avocado and unsalted nuts.

Essential fats

The two primary essential fats are Omega 3 and Omega 6. These fats are required to regulate blood viscosity (thickness), blood clotting, cholesterol, fat levels and water balance. It has been discovered that Omega 3 also plays a role in energy production. Omega 3 directs glucose to the muscles or liver for storage, and directs fat to be burned to produce heat as opposed to being stored. This double benefit of encouraging glucose storage and fat burning is important in conserving glucose for energy and getting rid of fat. Salmon, pumpkin seeds, hemp seeds and soya beans are good sources of Omega 3 and 6.

Saturated fat

A diet high in saturated fat increases the level of blood cholesterol. These fats are found primarily in animal foods such as cheese, fatty meats, cakes and biscuits and are generally hard at room temperature.

Protein

Proteins are essential for the growth and repair of all cells in the body. They play a crucial role in virtually all biological processes in the body. The three main functions of protein are:

1. Growth, development and repair of muscle tissues.
2. Regulation of metabolism through reactions controlled by enzymes.
3. An energy source when fat or carbohydrate stores are low.

Once protein enters the body it is broken down into amino acids, the building blocks of protein. There are 20 amino acids, of which nine are essential amino acids and the rest are non-essential. The non-essential amino acids are produced by the body, but the essential amino acids are not so they must be consumed in the diet.

Generally, proteins from animal sources, such as meat, poultry, fish, eggs, milk and cheese, are good sources of essential amino acids. Vegetable sources of protein tend to lack one or more of the essential amino acids. Vegetable sources can be combined (e.g. rice and beans, milk and wheat cereal, corn and beans) to include all the essential amino acids.

Amino acids

Proteins are made up of amino acids of which there are 20 (nine essential supplied by the diet only and 11 non-essential, which can be produced by the body). Together these combine to produce hundreds of different proteins. Each protein is made up of thousands of amino acids, which are broken down during digestion and reformed into the protein that the body requires.

The essential amino acids include: leucine, isoleucine, lysine, methionine, threonine, phenylalanine, tryptophane, valine and histidine.

Rugby is a power-based sport, which means that increases in lean muscle mass are desirable, requiring protein to be available in appropriate amounts in the diet. When players are trying to increase muscle mass they need to raise their protein intake.

Although protein provides an energy source when calories from fat or carbohydrate are deficient, it is not an ideal way of providing energy as it means that muscle growth is inhibited due to protein being used to provide energy instead. Protein cannot be stored for later use, unlike carbohydrate and fat, so if more protein is consumed than the body needs for growth and repair, the excess protein will either be broken down for energy or converted into fat and stored.

Fibre

Fibre is important to ensure the removal of waste products that occur as the result of digestion. It helps to slow digestion and the rate at which nutrients are absorbed; this produces a steady rather than a rapid release of glucose and as such controls blood sugar levels. Eating the correct amount of fruit/vegetables and a bran-based cereal will go a long way to providing the fibre required for a healthy diet.

Vitamins and minerals

Vitamins and minerals cannot be made by the body and have to be supplied through your diet. These essential nutrients help to prevent disease and assist in the production of energy, red blood cells and the growth and repair of muscles. The more you exercise, the more vitamins and minerals you require.

Fruit and vegetables provide the majority of the vitamins and minerals we need. As a guide 1–2 pieces of fruit and 4–5 portions of vegetables should be eaten each day. Vegetables that grow above the ground (beans, broccoli, peppers etc.) are higher in fibre than vegetables that grow below ground. The darker and brighter the colour of the vegetable, the greater its mineral and vitamin content.

A general multivitamin supplement can be taken to assist appropriate dietary needs; as with all supplements it should be taken to support, not replace, dietary intake.

The training diet for rugby

The most important dietary requirement for a rugby player in training is to consume a well-balanced, nutritionally complete diet that allows the player to train hard, recover from training and maintain a healthy body. Age, body size (composition), training levels and intensity should all be considered when planning a nutritional programme.

The training diet of a rugby player should be:

- High in energy to help with muscle gain. Eating three meals and regular snacks every day help to meet this goal.
- High in carbohydrate-rich foods such as bread, rice, pasta, breakfast cereal, bread, fruit and smoothies. These should form the basis for most meals and snacks. This will help with exercise performance, recovery from training and muscle gain.
- Low in fat, particularly if trying to reduce body fat. Include an appropriate amount of protein-rich foods such as meat, chicken, fish and dairy products.
- Include five portions of fruit and vegetables each day. These are needed for preventing illness, building muscles and repairing injury.
- Maintain adequate hydration. Keep alcohol intake to a minimum as it results in poor recovery and slow repair of injuries and contributes to excess weight.

Fuelling up with carbohydrates

A high-carbohydrate training diet is a must for optimum sports performance because it produces the biggest stores of muscle glycogen. The greater your glycogen stores are in your muscles, the longer you can exercise. Depletion of glycogen stores during training or a match will lead to fatigue, poor energy levels and reduced ability to recover from training sessions. In order for a player to meet the fuel requirements, carbohydrate intake before, during and after exercise is essential.

Table 9.2 Carbohydrate intake based on activity levels

Level of training	Carbohydrate requirements g/kg of body weight/day
Light – less than 1 hour/day	4–5 g
Light–moderate – 1–2 hours/day	5–6 g
Moderate – 2–3 hours/day	6–7 g
Heavy – more than 3 hours/day	8–10 g

Monitoring carbohydrate intake

You do not need to carry a set of scales around with you to ensure you are taking in the correct amount of carbohydrates. The following table provides information about the carbohydrate content of common foods. Each food provides 50 g of carbohydrate. Use this information to plan a daily menu, or specific pre-match meals and post-exercise recovery meals to meet the carbohydrate intake targets provided in table 9.2. These carbohydrate-rich foods should form the basis of meals and snacks, along with other nutrient-rich foods to balance the meal.

Table 9.3 Foods containing 50g of carbohydrate

Food type and quantity	Serving
100 g bread	3–4 slices
175 g boiled rice	4 tablespoons
200 g cooked pasta	8 tablespoons
60 g breakfast cereal	1 large bowl
Rice cakes	8
Apples/oranges/pears	3–4 medium
Bananas	2–3
70 g dried fruit e.g. raisins	2 tablespoons
500 ml fruit juice	500 ml
300 g boiled potato	5 small
175 g jacket potato	1 medium
330 g mashed potato	7 heaped tablespoons
1 litre milk	1 litre
425 g rice pudding	1 can
Jaffa cakes	6
Cereal bars	2–3
100 g currant buns	2
Malt loaf	3 slices
400 g baked beans/spaghetti	1 can
Isotonic sports drink	800 ml
Glucose or sugar	50 g

Source: The Dieticians in Sport and Exercise Nutrition (DISEN): www.disen.org

Timing and type of carbohydrate

Although the amount of carbohydrate in the diet is of primary importance, the type of carbohydrate may also have an impact on improving performance. In recent years the concept of the Glycaemic Index (GI) has been used in sports nutrition. The GI ranks carbohydrate foods according to their effect on blood glucose levels. The rise in blood glucose affects the body's insulin response to the food eaten and this will ultimately affect the fuel mix and carbohydrate stores available to the exercising muscles. For best performance it is useful to understand which carbohydrate foods have 'high GI' and 'low GI' values and when to eat them.

Glycaemic Index

This is a scale that describes the speed at which carbohydrate is converted into glucose in the blood. The index ranks foods between 0 and 100, with 0 being low and 100 high. Foods with a low index provide a slower, more gradual release of glucose into the blood, whereas those with a high index provide an almost immediate supply of glucose for a short period of time.

Glucose absorption rates

This graph illustrates the difference in the rate of glucose absorption between high and low GI food.

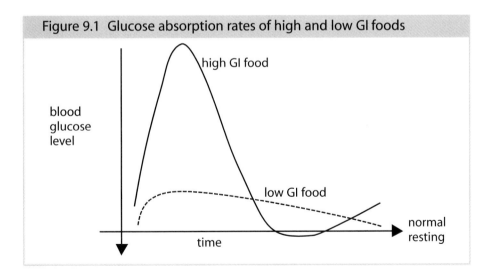

Figure 9.1 Glucose absorption rates of high and low GI foods

Source: Reddin, D. et al. (2003), *Nutritional Guidelines for England Players and Coaches*, RFU.

Table 9.4 Glycaemic index of certain foods

Food type	High (60–100)		Moderate (45–59)		Low (<45)	
Bread, grain and pulses	White rice	72	Pitta bread	57	Wholemeal pasta	42
	Noodles	70	White pasta	55	Chick peas	36
	White bread	70	Basmati rice	50	Kidney beans	30
	Wholemeal bread	69	Baked beans	48	Lentils	25
	Brown rice	60	Oats	49	Soya beans	20
			Spaghetti	45		
Breakfast cereals	Cornflakes	80	Porridge	48	All Bran	42
	Weetabix	75				
	Crunchy Nut	72				
	Special K	69				
	Shredded Wheat	67				
	Muesli	66				
Fruit	Watermelon	72	Pineapple	59	Grapes	44
	Raisins	68	Apricots	57	Oranges	40
	Melon	65	Bananas	55	Apples	36
			Mango	51	Pear	30
			Kiwi fruit	50	Peaches	22
					Plums	22
					Cherries	20
					Grapefruit	20
Vegetables	Parsnips (cooked)	98	Yams	51	Peas	40
	Chips	95	Sweet potatoes	48	Carrots (raw)	35
		95	Sweet corn	48	Green beans	10
	Baked potato	92			Aubergines	10
	Carrots (cooked)	85			Broccoli	10
	Mashed potato	75			Lettuce	10
	Pumpkin	70			Onions	10
	Turnip	70			Mushrooms	10
	New potato	70			Red peppers	10
					Tomatoes	10
					Cabbage	10
					Garlic	10
Other	Honey	87	Sugar	59	Yoghurt	36
	Rice cakes	85	Oatmeal biscuits	54	Ice cream	35
	Crackers	80	Marmalade	51	Whole milk	34
	Crisps	80	Sponge cake	46	Milk (semi-skimmed)	32
	Jelly beans	78				
	Chocolate bar	70			Peanuts	20
	Jam	65				
Drinks	Sports drinks	80	Fresh apple juice	40		
	Cordials	70	Fresh orange juice			
	Fizzy drinks	70		40		

GI values will vary for different manufacturers or if the food is cooked, fresh, ripe or raw. The figures in table 9.4 are approximate values and provide a basic guide to the value of the different food types.

Knowledge of the Gycaemic Index value of foods is important for the coach and player. Eating the right foods at the right times plays a major factor in ensuring the body has the correct fuel to perform and to recover. However, players need to feel comfortable with the drinks and foods they consume and therefore should not choose them based on the Glycaemic Index alone.

GI rules

Before exercise
Foods with a low GI (slow release) should be eaten 2–3 hours before training/playing to provide an energy store for performing.

During exercise
Moderate to high GI foods and drinks should be consumed.

After exercise
Foods with a high GI (quick release) should be eaten in the first hour after exercise to provide a rapid energy supply to replace the glycogen stores used up during exercise. A few hours after exercise meals and snacks should be comprised primarily of low rather than high GI foods.

Eating to perform

You should now have a better understanding of the basic principles of a well-balanced diet and why this is essential to ensure that training efforts are maximised. What players eat before training or in the lead-up to a game is of great importance as this is the fuel supply they will be relying on for their energy.

Pre-match or -training

- Aim to eat low to moderate GI foods before exercise to provide a more sustained source of carbohydrate.

- Have your last meal 2–3 hours before the game (e.g. cereal and toast, sandwiches, pasta with vegetable-based sauce) and possibly a light snack 1–2 hours before (e.g. banana, toast, cereal bar, drink).
- If you suffer from pre-game nerves or can't compete with a full stomach, try having nutritious drinks (e.g. smoothies) or eat early and top up with small snacks or drinks closer to the game.

Light meals/snack ideas pre-exercise or match
Porridge made with semi-skimmed milk
Cereal with low-fat milk, topped with a banana, juice to drink
Granary toast with margarine, jam or honey, glass of milk to drink
Chicken, ham or tuna sandwich and a piece of fruit
Cereal or muesli bar (some have a high fat content) and low-fat milkshake
Baked beans on toast or with jacket potato
Bagel with reduced fat cream cheese

During exercise

- It is important to top up fluid levels and carbohydrate during a game or training to minimise fatigue and help concentration.
- Drink during breaks in play.
- Drink some sports drinks in place of water to top up carbohydrate and fluid.
- At half-time, aim for 200–400 ml of sports drink or water. Carbohydrate gels can give an added boost to energy.

Post-match or -training

Inadequate refuelling after the game can lead to decreased energy during the following week of training. It can also slow down repair of injury. Start refuelling your energy stores as soon as you have finished exercising – if you wait too long your recovery will be delayed.

- Aim to consume about 1 g of carbohydrate per kg body weight within the first 1–2 hours after exercise. If you are doing only light exercise then 50 g of carbohydrate should be enough.
- Drinking and eating nutrient-rich carbohydrate foods with a moderate to high GI will provide a readily available source of carbohydrate for glycogen resynthesis, and these should be the major fuel choices as soon as possible after exercise.

- Rehydration is crucial to recovery and a carbohydrate drink can be used to assist this, as well as replenishing glycogen levels. It is likely that most players will have an alcoholic drink, but it is important that they begin the rehydration process prior to hitting the bar!
- For refuelling to be carried out effectively, the player will need to plan ahead. Although suitable food and drink may be provided at the training venue, it is useful to carry a selection of snacks in your kit bag.

Ideal refuelling foods containing 50 g of carbohydrate	
2 large bananas	2 Kellogg's Nutrigrain bars
3 slices thick-sliced bread	1 Muller rice
1 bagel	60 g breakfast cereal
2 slices malt loaf	8 tablespoons cooked pasta
330 ml bottle fruit smoothie	4 tablespoons rice
15 dried apricots	75 g (1 sheet) noodles
6 jaffa cakes	1 medium jacket potato
79–90 g chocolate-covered snack bar	8 tablespoons baked beans

Protein requirements for training

For players wishing to increase muscle mass it is important to remember that muscle is gained through a combination of resistance exercise and a diet containing adequate energy and carbohydrate to fuel the muscle. Protein is not critical for fuelling working muscles. When carbohydrate is in short supply, protein can be used as a fuel, but then it gets diverted from its more important role – growth and repair.

As a guide, for every 1 kg of bodyweight the player should eat between 1.4 and 1.8 g of protein. For example, if you are a rugby player weighing 85 kg you would require 119–153 g protein/day, which can easily be achieved by a balanced diet; protein supplements are not necessary to achieve this intake of protein.

Table 9.5 Sample match day menus

Time	Example 1	Example 2	Example 3
Breakfast 8.30 am	Scrambled eggs on wholegrain toast Orange juice	Beans on wholegrain toast Apple juice	Porridge or All Bran cereal with semi-skimmed milk Grapefruit juice
10.00 am	Glass of water		
Pre-match meal 12 noon	Tuna and small portion of wholemeal pasta with salad Glass of water	Chicken salad pitta bread wrap Low-fat yoghurt Glass of water	Chick peas with basmati rice and salad Glass of water
2 pm–3 pm	Regular intake of water and/or isotonic/hypotonic sports drink to maintain hydration and blood glucose levels Energy bar if required		
3 pm match			
Half-time			
5 pm post-match meal	Sports drink (protein:carbohydrate ratio 1:3) Players should be encouraged to drink first and then eat		
	To consist of: Chicken, ham, tuna, jam, honey and white bread sandwiches or rolls Jacket potatoes or bagels with a protein topping Jaffa cakes, meal replacement bars, dried fruit or bananas		
7.30 pm evening meal	Chicken and small portion of brown rice Steamed mixed vegetables Glass of water	Tuna wholemeal pasta bake with sweetcorn and broccoli Glass of water	Spaghetti and tomato-based sauce with quorn Glass of water

Table 9.6 Protein requirements for different activity levels

Activity levels	Protein requirements g/kg of body weight/day
Non-athletes	0.75–0.8 g
Strength and speed athletes	1.4–1.8 g
Endurance athletes	1.2–1.4 g

Although some resistance-trained athletes and bodybuilders consume protein in excess of 2–3g/kg bodyweight, there is no evidence that such high intakes enhance the response to training or increase the gains in muscle mass and strength. While such diets are not necessarily harmful, they are expensive and can fail to meet other nutritional goals such as ensuring adequate carbohydrate to optimise training and performance.

Protein supplements

The busy lives of players today are a major reason for many dietary deficiencies. Protein shakes are often used to meet dietary demand because of the convenience of taking the protein in drink form. Failure to consume adequate amounts of protein when training frequency and intensity is high will result in the desired increase in strength and size not taking place.

A benefit of supplements is that they are generally in liquid form and require less digestion than solid food. This means they are absorbed more rapidly, which is especially beneficial post-training when we are looking to return the body to above its normal state to encourage growth and recovery. Supplements should be taken to complement your regular meals and should not be a substitute for them.

Table 9.7 Foods containing 20 g of protein

Food type and quantity	Serving
75 g lean beef/lamb/pork	2 medium slices
75 g turkey/chicken	1 small breast
100 g salmon/tuna	1 small can
100 g grilled fish	1 small fillet
Eggs	3 medium
75 g cheddar cheese	2 matchbox-size pieces
150 g cottage cheese	1 small carton
600 ml semi-skimmed milk	1 pint
400 g baked beans	1 can

Table 9.8 Foods containing 10 g of protein

Food type and quantity	Serving
100 g bread	3–4 slices
250 g pasta/noodles	8 tbsp (cooked)
100 g cornflakes	2 large bowls
100 g wheat biscuits	5 biscuits
200 g yoghurt	1 small pot
50 g nuts or seeds	4 tablespoons
150 g kidney beans/lentils	5 tbsp (cooked)
250 g tofu (soya bean curd)	1 packet

Source: The Dieticians in Sport and Exercise Nutrition (DISEN): www.disen.org

Gaining lean mass or losing body fat

For certain positions, most notably the front row, it is more acceptable to have a higher amount of body fat. This is due to the benefits that weight has in this position. Ideally, the weight should be provided by lean muscle and as such it is generally more important to gain lean muscle or lose body fat rather than just gaining or losing weight. As with most things in rugby and conditioning, quality over quantity is the critical factor.

Roy Heady is the Head of Sports Science at the RFU and often has to work with players who are looking to gain lean muscle mass or reduce their body fat. He believes the key to a successful diet is to make players aware of how to bring about the desired results, and then work on ensuring this behaviour becomes a habit. Keeping to a good diet is a skill, and like passing needs to be practised until flaws have been ironed out and the correct techniques learned. He believes that coaches, parents and partners have an import role to play in reinforcing this regime and need to be educated in order to assist the player to develop these positive eating habits.

Top tips for losing weight (body fat)

- To lose weight you must create a negative energy balance by burning off more calories than you consume. Reduce the total fat content of the diet, although you will still require the glycogen from carbohydrates for exercising.
- Increasing muscle mass raises your basal metabolic rate (calories you use doing nothing). Thus, higher muscle content results in greater calorie consumption

throughout the day as muscles are more metabolically active than fat.

- Weight training and varied intensity aerobic activity should be undertaken to reduce fat storage.
- Alcohol encourages fat storage as it cannot be stored in the body and has to be converted into ATP (energy). While this is occurring, fat is not being used and thus more is stored. Alcohol intake should therefore be reduced.
- A balanced diet is the most effective way of losing body fat, combined with regular exercise. Rapid weight loss of more than $\frac{1}{2}$ kg a week tends to be the result of lean muscle being lost.

Top tips for gaining weight (lean muscle)

- Heavy resistance training stimulates the greatest muscle growth.
- You need adequate rest and recovery in order to increase lean muscle mass.
- You need a positive energy balance – consuming more calories than you burn off. Without this, lean weight gain will not occur.
- An increase of 500 calories a day is generally required to promote weight gain.
- This increase should come from carbohydrate and protein foods.
- Eat a protein and carbohydrate based meal in the first hour after exercise to promote growth and recovery.
- Eat every three to four hours and five or six times a day; this ensures that energy levels are maintained.
- Drink a glass of milk with all meals.
- Make cottage cheese your friend – use it as a snack or blend it into a shake at night to provide a large quantity of slow-release proteins while you sleep.
- Get yourself a selection of small Tupperware dishes (250 cm^2 size) and fill four or five with snacks for every day: raw nuts, diced grilled chicken or lean steak, 'leftovers' from high-protein meals (always cook a bit extra), tinned tuna with lemon juice or fresh herbs.
- Buy snacks in bulk so you always have a supply – 1 kg bags of nuts, 1 litre tubs of cottage cheese and so on.

Hydration

Exercising causes the body to produce heat, as a result of which we sweat to remove it and to prevent body temperature from rising excessively. The increased rate of breathing also results in more fluid being lost as water vapour as part of the respiratory process. Failing to replace this fluid loss will result in the increased onset of fatigue and dehydration, which limits performance and can also have serious health implications such as heat stroke.

Monitoring fluid loss

Body weight
Players should be weighed before and after playing and training. This will establish the amount of body weight lost through sweating and provides information that can be used to establish hydration strategies. During matches or intense training it is not uncommon for players to lose between 2 and 4 kg of body weight.

Urine colour
Players should monitor the colour of their urine as this provides a good guide to their hydration levels. A light-yellow coloured urine and a high volume indicates that hydration levels are close to the desired state. Dark yellow urine and low volume indicate that fluid levels need to be increased. Urine colour charts can be put up in toilets to help educate players and encourage them to monitor their hydration levels in this manner.

Managing fluid loss and replacement

The loss of body fluid decreases blood volume and causes blood to thicken (viscosity). This requires the heart and lungs to work harder in order to transport blood around the body. As a result it is more difficult to maintain the intensity of effort while training or playing and performance can suffer. A drop in fluid levels of two or three per cent will seriously affect your aerobic capabilities and also result in a reduction in the ability to produce power and speed.

Hydration strategy

Be well hydrated before exercising. If you wait until you are thirsty before you drink, you are already in the early stages of dehydration. The more you are exercising the more you need to drink, although this should not be forced. An adult who is exercising should be drinking 2–4 litres of water a day depending on their size – as a guide, 40 ml of fluid/kg of body weight should be consumed through the day. For example, an 85 kg centre should consume about 3.4 litres in a day.

Drinking half a litre of water two hours before exercise will help to raise hydration levels. This can be topped up with regular drinks from a water bottle before and during exercise.

Players should have regular access to fluid during training and games. It is recommended that 150–350 ml of fluid should be consumed every 15–20 minutes (American College of Sports Medicine, 2000). During exercise it is appropriate to use a carbohydrate sports drink to help replenish fluid levels as this has the additional benefit of providing an energy source. The sodium content of these drinks also plays a positive role in preventing muscle cramp as salt loss through sweating is being at least partially replaced.

Heat and cold

If training in extreme heat, sweat loss will be increased and hydration strategies need to be adjusted accordingly. In cold weather players will still lose a similar amount of sweat, but during cold conditions players tend to drink less, making them more susceptible to dehydration.

After exercise, you should consume between 1 and 1½ litres of fluid for every kg of body weight lost during exercise in order to return the body to its pre-exercise state. This should be done gradually as consuming fluid in large quantities too quickly can be dangerous. As a guide, 600–800 ml can be absorbed by the body per hour and this will safely and effectively restore fluid levels.

A carbohydrate-based sports drink can aid this process as well as assisting glycogen replacement. These drinks generally contain sodium, which encourages greater fluid consumption. Water dilutes the sodium content in blood and reduces the urge to drink; this means players may stop drinking before they are fully rehydrated.

Hyponatraemia

Consuming water too rapidly and in large quantities leads to increased plasma levels in the blood, resulting in reduced blood pressure and oxygen transportation. In severe cases this can have serious health consequences.

Sports drinks

These drinks have two prime functions: to replace fluid levels and to provide a supply of carbohydrate (glucose) as a source of energy. The content of the drinks determines how effectively it performs each of these two functions. The more carbohydrate a drink contains, the greater its ability to act as an energy source. The higher the carbohydrate concentration (more particles), the rate at which it is absorbed into the bloodstream slows, reducing its effectiveness as a fluid replacement drink. Drinks with a low carbohydrate concentration are absorbed more rapidly from the gut into the bloodstream. This enables them to replace fluid levels rapidly but with lessened effectiveness in replacing energy stores.

Water should still be the prime method of fluid replacement, but mixing its intake with an appropriate sports drink has additional benefits. Water is not always easy to drink due to its taste and can cause some players to feel bloated. Sports drinks, as well as having physiological benefits, are also more pleasant tasting and are often easier to drink than water.

Hypotonic

These drinks have a carbohydrate level of less than 4 g/100 ml. This concentration is lower than the osmolality (particle concentration) of body fluid, and as such hypotonic drinks are rapidly absorbed from the gut into the bloodstream. These drinks are absorbed more quickly than water alone and provide a good hydration source with some benefits as an energy replacement.

Usage: best when the need is to replace fluid without great need for energy.

Isotonic

These drinks share a similar concentration level as body fluid so are absorbed at least as quickly as water. Their carbohydrate content ranges between 4 and 8 g/100 ml, so as well as the quick absorption rate into the bloodstream they offer a good energy source as well.

Usage: these are the most commonly used type of sports drink that can be used before, during or after exercise as they meet fluid and energy needs well.

Hypertonic

The concentration levels of these drinks are higher than body fluid and as such take longer to be absorbed from the gut into the bloodstream. Carbohydrate levels are above 8 g/100 ml and so these drinks provide a high energy source. The greater concentration means absorption takes longer in comparison to water, hypotonic and isotonic drinks, which makes these drinks less effective as a fluid replacement drink.

Usage: generally used to aid recovery from exercise.

If choosing a fluid replacement drink then hypotonic- or isotonic-style drinks are more effective. Both these types of drink also supply carbohydrate for energy, with isotonic the more effective. Isotonic drinks are a good choice as they are highly effective as both a fluid and energy source. Hypertonic drinks will provide greater levels of carbohydrate for energy, but do not contribute to fluid replacement as effectively as the other drinks.

Drinks should be served cooled as this makes them easier to consume, which encourages fluid intake. They should be drunk from a sports bottle with a teat or straw; the fluid should not be held in the mouth in order to reduce the chance of erosion of tooth enamel.

Table 9.9 Examples of the different types of sports drinks

Hypotonic	Isotonic	Hypertonic
Lucozade Hydro Active (2 g carbs/100 ml)	Lucozade Sport (6.4 g carbs/100 ml)	Lucozade Energy (17.2 g carbs/100 ml)

These sports drinks are generally quite expensive, but it is relatively straightforward to make your own at a fraction of the price with some readily available ingredients.

Table 9.10 Home-made sports drinks

Hypotonic	Isotonic	Hypertonic
100 ml fruit cordial 900 ml water 1 g/pinch of salt Drink chilled or 250 ml fruit juice 750 ml water 1 g/pinch of salt Drink chilled	200ml fruit cordial 800 ml water 1 g/pinch of salt Drink chilled or 500 ml fruit juice 500 ml water 1 g/pinch of salt Drink chilled	400 ml fruit cordial 600 ml water 1 g/pinch of salt Drink chilled or 750 ml fruit juice 250 ml water 1 g/pinch of salt Drink chilled

Source: Bean, A. (2003), *The Complete Guide to Sports Nutrition* (4th Edition), A & C Black, London.

Nutrition and LTAD

Regardless of age, a well-balanced diet is essential to promote health and well-being. The number of children classified as clinically obese has never been greater and it is crucial that care is taken to ensure good dietary habits are learned at an early age. When training volume and intensity increase as players progress through the LTAD pathway, they need to be educated in this area and ensure they have the correct fuel to perform.

Summary

As coaches we should explore every possible means of enhancing our players' and team's performance. This might involve repeatedly watching videos of opponents, one-to-one skill sessions or personalised conditioning programmes. However, very little if any time is set aside to ensure that players are eating correctly and taking on board appropriate fluids. These are the building blocks on which performance is based, for without the right fuels your players will be unable to achieve the standards that their talent or application warrant.

Educating your players in this area is especially important when you consider the busy lifestyles that many lead. Failing to monitor and support their nutritional intake can only have a negative effect on performance, and detracts from the good work that you may be carrying out in other areas of player development. As a coach you will at least be able to influence the nutritional habits of players on match and training days by developing a hydration strategy during the day and setting the post-match/training menu to aid recovery. These minor changes will help support the education of players and will begin to spread to other aspects of their diet.

CHAPTER 10

Preparation and recovery

This chapter will examine some strategies and methods coaches can use pre- and post-match to help players to achieve peak performance. Whereas coaches pay a great deal of attention to the organisation of their training sessions in the week leading into a match, they can sometimes leave things to chance on match day itself – however, not structuring the events properly on the day can severely reduce the likelihood of success.

Ask coaches what pre-match preparation is and most will say a warm-up; however, this is the bare minimum that should take place prior to performance. Pre-event there is a great deal that needs to be done in order to ensure that teams and players are appropriately prepared for the contest. If pre-event preparation is limited, post-match recovery is virtually non-existent. A token two-minute cool-down, to which neither coach nor player is fully committed, is the best that most clubs offer in this respect.

All recovery work is actually the first preparation session for the next training activity, and it is vitally important to ensure training time is utilised to its full poten-tial. It is up to the coach to set the standard in this area and stress the need for cool-downs to be completed correctly. Once this approach is set up and carried through then recovery work will become as accepted as the warm-up activity.

Match day preparation

It is important to establish a routine on match day that players are comfortable with and have had some role in developing. This gives them ownership and responsibility on the day and will help to ensure that they follow it through. Having a settled preparation routine will help players to relax, bring a more professional approach and ensure mental and physical preparation is of an appropriate nature.

Preparation should really begin the night before a game, as it is important that players receive enough good quality sleep (8–10 hours), have an appro-priate meal and are well hydrated (see Chapter 9). Players should eat breakfast and have a pre-match meal 2 to 3 hours before kick-off to allow digestion to take place. When travelling on long away journeys it is important that players do not rely on service station food for their pre-match meal. Appropriate food and liquid should be provided for the journey to ensure that energy levels are maintained through the correct sources. A tuna or chicken pasta salad is a better meal for the journey than a pasty and crisps from the service station. On long away journeys it is worth having a stop and performing some light warm-up and ball-handling activity to relieve the boredom of the journey and to pro-vide mental and physical stimulation.

Before kick-off

Clive Woodward has stated that England's success as a team was due to atten-tion to detail at all levels – playing, administration, coaching and management. His philosophy was that doing 100 things one per cent better can bring about great improvements in performance. This does not mean that you as a coach should personally take care of everything, as you have enough to worry about with direct preparation for the match. There is, however, a need for you to ensure that the little things are taken care of on match day. Developing set roles and responsibilities for physiotherapists, groundsperson, treasurer, chairperson, bar manager or whoever will provide a cohesive back-room team. This professional and organised feel will transmit through the club and players and requires only minimal planning. It will take pressure off the players and allow the coach to concentrate on the game – not putting up the post protectors when he should be conducting the pre-match pep talk.

Do not underestimate the benefits to the team that having a clean changing room – laundered shirts hung up and so on – can have. By removing variables that can bring about stress on match day, you will create an environment in which players are more likely to perform.

As a coach it is important to provide direction on match day to help focus players' minds on the task at hand. A good way of doing this is to produce a timetable for the pre-match preparation that can be put up in the changing room. This ensures players are aware of what is going on and their part in this process. As a coach there is nothing worse than trying to start a warm-up with players still receiving treatment, going to the toilet, still changing or chatting to their boy/girlfriend. Use senior players to ensure that timings are kept to as preparation time is limited before kick-off – a timetable helps to ensure this period is used most effectively.

Table 10.1 Sample match day timetable

Time	Event
1.00	Meet – treatment times decided
1.10	Strapping and personal physical/mental preparation
2.00	Referee's instructions
2.05	Team tactics/goals
2.15	Outside for team warm-up
2.50	Back inside for final personal preparation and instructions
3.00	Kick-off

It is important to work with your physiotherapist to give time slots to players to receive their strapping or treatment. This way the players and physiotherapist are aware of who should be where and when. You should also arrange a time with the referee to talk to the players, to make his/her checks and conduct the coin toss. Ideally, this should be done before the warm-up as it can be frustrating and distracting to have to stop the warm-up to allow the referee to speak to the players. Referees are in the habit of doing this because of time constraints and poorly organised teams, so it is up to coaches to create a situation where this does not occur and where the referee's needs are met without impinging on team preparation.

Tactical preparation and game plans should be devised and worked on in the week during training sessions. Prior to kick-off, these should be reinforced through visual cues in the dressing room and brief instruction from the coach(es). However, reality dictates that it is often necessary in the warm-up to run through moves with new players, although this is far from ideal. The warm-up is for preparing the body and mind for the contest – having to run through plays demonstrates a lack of preparation and can undermine confidence.

Warming up

Recent research (Boyle, 2004) suggests that static stretching may not be the most appropriate activity for warm-ups. This flies in the face of what most coaches have been advocating and carrying out for years, but there is some sound logic behind this. We are not saying that stretching should not be carried out, only that there are more appropriate stretches that should be used. Dynamic stretching involves stretching the muscle by lengthening and contracting it. This is different from static stretching, which lengthens the muscle and maintains this length for usually 10–20 seconds.

It is also argued that dynamic stretching replicates movements in rugby more closely than static stretching, and as such is a more relevant method of preparing the body for exercise. The evidence also suggests that static stretching actually reduces the force productivity of muscles, as the excessive lengthening reduces the muscle's capacity to execute explosive actions. The opposite is the case for dynamic stretching, which increases the force generated in the muscles and as such prepares them for the explosive movements of the game.

Your match day warm-up should be practised prior to matches so players are aware of what they will be doing on the day of the game. Learning new drills and routines can negatively effect performance as players will most likely only perform them with a moderate degree of success.

Why warm up?

Warming up:
- raises body core and muscle temperature, preparing each for exercise;
- provides mental stimulation and focus for exercise;
- increases metabolic rate, which means that energy production rises so that there is no sudden jump in the demand for energy when the game/training begins;
- raises heart rate and blood flow, resulting in oxygen being more readily available for use by the muscles;

- reduces the risk of soft tissue injury as muscles and connective tissue have been contracting in similar patterns to the movements required to generate high force during the game;
- increases muscle and nerve contraction, resulting in messages being sent with greater speed through the central nervous system, enabling muscles to act on them with greater speed and force.

Rugby is multi-directional, with jumping, turning, sprinting, pushing, pulling and grappling actions, and the warm-up should therefore include these to fully prepare the player for the contest.

Sample match day warm-up

2–3 min:	Handling and ball manipulation in a 20 m × 20 m grid
2–3 min:	Light aerobic activity (walking, jogging, skipping, bounding, slow/medium-paced multi-directional running)
2–3 min:	Low-intensity dynamic flexibility (see chapter 6)
2–3 min:	Handling/decision making 2 v 1/4 v 2 v 1)
2–3 min:	Dynamic flexibility
2–3 min:	Striding and bounding (10–20 m)
1 min:	Handling (5 m × 10 m channel in 4s handling ball)
2–3 min:	Dynamic flexibility (upper body and leg swings/thrusts)
2–3 min:	Sprinting (10–20 m, vary start positions)
2–3 min:	Contact preparation (spin away from shield, drive shield, burst through shield, light wrestling)
3–4 min:	Defensive work (realignment and communication)
3–4 min:	Offensive work (8 v 2 v 3 v 2 – defenders with shields)
8–10 min	Before kick-off go back inside and allow time for final instruction and preparation

---

This warm-up might require a bit more planning and practice than the traditional approach of pulse raiser, stretching and rugby work in set blocks, but it does better reflect the demands of the game and as a result is a more relevant method of preparing for the contest.

Be sure to allow players their own personal time and space to prepare themselves mentally for the game. Players will all have different ways of psyching themselves up – not all players need to head-butt the changing-room door to demonstrate their focus.

Warm-up drop-off

The positive effects of a warm-up reduce gradually when there is a period of inactivity and coaches should be aware that almost all of the benefits of the warm-up will be lost within 15 minutes. Therefore, in the period prior to kick-off players should be conducting their own physical/mental preparation to ensure this does not occur.

During the match

After kick-off

It is important to ensure that your substitutes are properly prepared and ready to enter the action at a moment's notice. It is worth devising some activities that these players can carry out in the dead ball areas to prepare them for the intensity of the game. This should include dynamic stretching, footwork, ball handling/decision making, collision management and position-specific skills. When possible, you should let the players know that they will be coming on so they can ensure that they are fully prepared.

Half-time

At half-time the coach has a limited opportunity to assess how the game is progressing and make any changes to rectify problems. It is also an important time to ensure that players are physically and mentally prepared for the second half. The first thing you should do is ensure that players are rehydrating and that those needing attention from the physio are catered for. This may take a couple of minutes and it is desirable not to have a formal team talk until all the players have had a drink, treatment, their heart rates have slowed and the adrenalin levels reduced. By doing this you are increasing the likelihood of the players listening and understanding. They will be focusing solely on you and be mentally, physically and emotionally in a more controlled state.

Do not try to give players too many instructions at half-time – they will not be able to cope with the information and you will end up diluting the importance of your message. Concentrate on two or three key areas that you want improved or continued focus upon; use questioning to ensure that the players are clear on these points. Some coaches appoint leaders within the team to provide feedback on defence or set-piece play, for example. They can then tell the team how these areas are operating and any adjustments that should be made as a result. This helps to empower the players as decision makers and makes them think about why things are happening rather than blindly following instructions.

If the half-time break is long enough (10 minutes is the maximum break but it can be less, so confirm the length of the break with the referee before the kick-off) there is nothing wrong with going back to the dressing room. It removes a number of distractions, and the visual cues and whiteboards can be utilised to stress tactical points. In bad weather it also makes good sense to be in a warm dressing room as opposed to on an open field.

After the match

After the final whistle

At the end of the game, once the appropriate post-match pleasantries have been exchanged, the team should be put through a structured cool-down. It is important to return the team gradually to its normal resting state – during this time players should begin the rehydration process.

Why cool down?

- Suddenly stopping exercising prevents blood flow back to the heart and can result in blood pooling in the legs. Light exercise results in blood being distributed to the brain and other body parts.
- Stretching promotes blood flow and helps to restore normal range of movement due to increased body temperature.
- Reduces the risk of delayed onset of muscle soreness (DOMS) by assisting with the removal of lactic acid.
- Promotes relaxation by reducing emotional arousal and returning the nervous system to its normal state.

Cool-down structure

- Light, aerobic activity (walking, jogging, skipping, bounding, slow-paced multi-directional running).
- Gentle dynamic stretching (as for the warm-up but at a lower intensity).
- Static stretching (hold stretches for between 15 and 30 seconds). There is a case for these stretches being conducted an hour or so after playing for maximum benefit.

Lactic Acid – produced in the main as a result of energy production through anaerobic glycolysis, when glycogen is broken down without oxygen to meet the body's energy needs. The accumulation of lactic acid then limits further energy production without the presence of oxygen. Oxygen prevents the chemical reaction that produces lactic acid from occurring. Warming down promotes blood flow, bringing oxygen into the cells and allowing lactic acid to be removed to the liver where it is converted back into glucose. Short duration activity (a few seconds) does not produce lactic acid as glycogen is not used (phosphocreatine provides the energy). Reducing the intensity of exercise results in more oxygen being available to the muscles to remove the lactic acid – this is known as repaying the oxygen debt.

Once the cool-down is complete and the players are back in the dressing room, there should be access to food and drink to aid their recovery process. Some feedback can be provided now in regards to the performance, though this should be fairly basic. A more detailed analysis and debriefing should take place at the following training session when there has been time to reflect and analyse the performance, tape and statistics. Players should also receive treatment for their injuries from the physiotherapist at this point, and appointments should be set for further treatment as appropriate.

Delayed Onset of Muscle Soreness (DOMS) is usually felt 24–48 hours after exercise and is the result of inflammation around the muscle or damage to the muscle fibre caused by exercise. It is most common when performing eccentric muscle actions (extending/lengthening the muscle) such as running downhill or eccentric (negative) weight training when the weight is lowered slowly and returned to the start position with assistance from a spotter. DOMS often occurs when you have not exercised for a length of time and then perform new or high-intensity activity with which the muscles are unfamiliar.

Contrast showers and ice baths

The use of ice baths and contrast showers is becoming more commonplace at all levels of sport to assist recovery. Having appropriate space and resources to carry out ice baths might be beyond most rugby clubs, but the use of contrast showers is a readily available alternative. The cold water (or ice) helps to reduce swelling, promotes recovery and helps to return body temperature to normal. Switching between cold and hot water causes increased vaso-constriction (prevents blood flow, reducing swelling) followed by vasodilation (increased blood flow, which aids the removal of waste products and brings oxygen and nutrients to the area). The process also increases the actions of the internal organs, which stimulates the functioning of the immune system.

To utilise this technique players should alternate between two or three minutes of hot water followed by 30 seconds of cold. This should be repeated three or four times. Do not put your head under the cold shower, always finish with a hot shower and dry and change immediately.

This process should be avoided by players with high blood pressure or circulatory problems.

The day after the match

It is important that players do not drink alcohol to excess following the high levels of exertion and have had an appropriate amount and type of food to assist recovery. It is essential to have 8–10 hours sleep, as the majority of the physical and psychological recovery takes place while we are sleeping. This will promote the repair of muscle fibres that are stretched and damaged during activity, and restore the energy-producing enzymes that are broken down during playing or training to produce energy.

Alcohol reduces the production (synthesis) of protein and as a result delays the growth and repair of muscles after exercise. It also has a diuretic effect, causing the body to excrete urine more regularly, thus promoting dehydration. Alcohol is high in calories, but cannot be used during exercise by the muscles to produce energy as only the liver can break down alcohol. The liver performs this function at a fixed speed and you cannot undo the effects of drinking by performing exercise.

Recovery should be designed to return the body to and then above the normal state; in this way the body has excess energy stores that can then be used to bring about improvements in training and muscle growth. Failing to properly replenish nutrient levels immediately after training delays recovery and ultimately prevents improvement in athletic performance.

The day following intense training or a match players should be encouraged to undertake a recovery session. This should be a low-intensity session designed to facilitate repair by removing waste products, helping to improve flexibility and returning muscles to their pre-exercise length. These sessions are commonly held in swimming pools as the water supports body weight (buoyancy), reducing the stress placed on the body/joints, and assists in the development of range of motion (flexibility at joints).

Sample recovery session

Players should have a water bottle by the pool for rehydration. This session can be adapted to be performed individually.

Warm-up: (11–16 minutes)
6 v 2 keep ball – 3–5 minutes
In the shallow end the six players have a ball (any shape) which they must keep away from the two defenders. They cannot catch the ball, but must use flicks and pushes to transfer it away from the defenders. If the ball is intercepted or hits the water, the player responsible swims a width and then swaps roles with a defender.

Handling: 2–3 minutes
In fives, jog and pass ball along line – players can perform miss, switch, loop etc. as they wish.

Dynamic stretching: 2–3 minutes
Players perform various dynamic stretches in a circle.

Static stretching: 4–5 minutes
Players perform various static stretches on the pool side. Mats should ideally be available for these stretches. Hold stretches for 10–15 seconds.

Main session: (10–15 minutes)
Two lengths of slow front crawl.
Perform the following exercises for 20 seconds each:

- Holding side of pool, crawl leg kick.
- Up to neck in water, perform chest flyes (pec deck).
- Stand facing side of pool and perform alternating leg hamstring curls.
- Sit on side of pool and perform alternating leg extensions.

Three minutes of jogging in the pool (aqua-jogging devices can be used).
Use various arm actions: punching, swing across body and small punches above head.
One-minute speed-skater action.

Balance and proprioception: (2–3 minutes)
One knee out of water, balance with eyes closed – 20 seconds.
One-leg hop, ¼ turns with eyes closed – perform clockwise and anticlockwise.

Cool-down: (5 minutes)
Walking width forwards and backwards.
Mixture of dynamic stretches.
On the pool side perform a variety of static stretches held for 20 seconds.

Tools for preparing and reviewing performance

Many coaches video matches and record the outcomes of set pieces, tackles made/missed, ball carries, metres gained and so on. This is a very valid method of carrying out a statistical analysis of the game and does provide many valuable conclusions in regards to performance. However, as this evaluation process is based around the game itself, coaches need to look a little further than this for answers to some of the questions that game analysis throws up.

The reason a player is less effective could be due to the preparation/training/lifestyle followed in the lead-up to the game. As such, it is important to monitor what players are doing in the build-up to matches, as this can allow them to establish a routine that allows them to perform more effectively on match day. Players and coaches must be aware of the need for appropriate preparation and be able to identify how this can influence performance. Players should be empowered in this process and, with correct education, can police themselves and adjust their activity in the build-up to matches to ensure their preparation is appropriate.

Players and coaches (team talk, organisation, substitutions, pre-match environment etc.) should also review their performance in matches, setting goals for future performance in order to assist continued improvement.

Sample player's evaluation form

Preparation
Players need to monitor their preparation to see how this is influencing performance.

Week before
Ranking the following areas on a sliding scale of 1 to 10 might help players to answer these questions more effectively (1 = poor, 10 = excellent).

Training: how well did your training go this week?

Psychology: what mental preparation did you use in the week?

Nutrition: ideally players should be following a guide diet and be aware of the types of food they should be eating and in what quantities.

Lifestyle: sleep/work/socialising.

Match day
Sleep: hours and quality of sleep?

Nutrition: when and what did you eat?

Psychology: what mental preparation did you use on match day?

What worked well in the build-up to the match?

How did you handle your emotions before and during the match?

What would you change in your preparation as a result of this review?

Post-match review
It is important that your players review their performances and compare them with the goals they have set for that match; these should relate to their longer-terms goals set through the performance profile.

When?
The review process should not take place immediately after the game; emotions will be running high and could result in you being over-critical of some areas and over-complimentary of others. Give yourself time to reflect objectively on what has occurred.

> **Post-match review process**
>
> **Goals**
>
> Set goals before each match that can be measured and that link to your long-term goals, set in your performance profile. These should not always be linked to the result of the match; set goals for effort, passing, tackling, positioning, throwing in, kicking etc. Measuring performance rather than result is vital to improving as a player.

Preparation/recovery and LTAD

As players move through the LTAD pathway the need to follow an appropriate preparation and recovery programme increases due to the intensity and volume of training. The fundamental principles of warming up and cooling down remain the same regardless of age, but the activities included will need to be altered to reflect the stage of development.

Summary

In this chapter we have highlighted the value that appropriate preparation and recovery can bring to your team's performance. Without addressing these areas, players will not be suitably prepared to perform and will not gain the most from their training as bodies have not recovered from previous exertion. There are a number of simple measures that have been discussed and can be implemented with minimal effort to bring about improvements in this area. By taking short cuts in preparation and recovery there is a good chance that you will come up short when it matters most.

Injury management and prevention

Rugby is a full-contact sport, although this description probably does not illustrate graphically enough the nature of a game where coaches stress the need to win the 'collision' or make 'big hits'.

It would be impossible to eradicate totally the potential for injury within rugby – by nature all sport has an element of risk. This does not mean, however, we should shrug our shoulders and accept it as an unavoidable hazard of the game. There are a number of things that coaches can do in order to minimise the likelihood of injury occurring. Being aware of the types of injury most commonly suffered in rugby, and how they occur, can enable preventative strategies to be implemented to ensure that players receive the best preparation for playing.

In order to prevent injuries it is important to know a little bit about the structure of the body, the type of injuries it is susceptible to, and how these occur in rugby.

Structure of the body

Muscles

There are over 400 skeletal muscles in the body that account for up to 50 per cent of our body weight. Muscles perform a number of important functions including creating force for movement and breathing, postural support and the production of heat. Muscles are attached to tendons, which in turn are attached to bones.

Tendons

Muscles are attached to the bone by tendons, which facilitate movement by concentrating the pull of the muscle on a small part of the bone. Tendons have a poor blood supply and as a result are generally slow to repair when injured.

Ligaments

These join bone to bone to strengthen and stabilise joints and to limit joint movement in certain directions. When ligaments are damaged the stability of the joint is reduced.

Cartilage

Cartilage helps to reduce the friction between bones when they come into contact at a joint, as well as acting as a shock absorber. Cartilage has no blood vessels or nerves and, if damaged, heals very slowly.

The basics of injury prevention

Preventative strategies – pre-habilitation rather than re-habilitation

Many of the strategies that coaches and athletes can implement to reduce the likelihood of injury are fairly straightforward. What prevents this from happening is a sense of false economy, a belief that the time taken to perform these strategies is time that cannot be spared because of the need for 'fitness and conditioning' or technical training. The reality is that preventative work is a vital part of 'fitness and conditioning'. A small outlay of time in this area will pay a great dividend in terms of producing better athletes and reducing the amount of time lost throughout the season due to injury.

Quantity and intensity of training/matches

The amount, type and intensity of training and matches that players are involved in is a major factor in determining their exposure to injury. When the body is in a fatigued state, the muscles' effectiveness in protecting their associated connective tissues is reduced, increasing the risk of damage to bone, cartilage, tendons and ligaments. Appropriate hydration and nutritional intake before and during training/playing can reduce the onset of fatigue and hence the risk of injury.

Training or playing when fatigued increases the risk of injury. A simple self-test to assess well-being is for players to record their heart rate every morning upon waking. If there is a fluctuation of 10 beats from their normal rate, this is an indication that their body is not in its normal state and they should not train that day.

A reduction in the intensity and volume of training (tapering) at planned stages of the periodised year needs to be employed to allow sufficient time for recovery and growth. As players are more likely to be injured when playing matches or taking part in full-contact training, the amount of matches and contact sessions needs to be carefully monitored.

This is especially the case with adolescents, whose bodies are undergoing major changes in their physical growth. Young players are often under pressure to play for school, club and representative teams, and regularly play two or three games in a week. This places them at a greater risk of injury and reduces the amount of time available for skill and tactical training, which is crucial in developing them as players. The Youth Structured Season has been designed to provide appropriate time for the development of skills and reduce the possibility of overplaying; it is therefore crucial that coaches utilise those days without matches for skill development, rather than seeking out an extra fixture.

Muscle weakness

Too often players begin a training phase without being properly prepared to do so. Plyometrics and weight training are two prime examples of activities that should only be introduced after technical and body preparedness sessions. First, players should be assessed to see if they are physically able to cope with a particular type of training; second, it is vital that the appropriate techniques are taught and observed.

Appropriate warm-up and cool-down

An appropriate warm-up will reduce muscle stiffness, which has a direct relationship to the risk of injury. Cooling down after exercise helps to remove lactic acid that has built up during exercise; it also increases the supply of oxygen to the muscles, which helps to return them to their pre-exercise state. This will help to prevent muscle soreness in the days following exercise and assist the recovery process from exercise.

Massage

If you are training and competing on a regular basis, a regular visit to a sports masseur is money well spent. Training places the muscles under repeated strain and can lead to knots developing as the fibres become joined together. Poor technique and lack of sleep can also produce the same effects. These knots prevent the muscles from functioning correctly or to their full potential, which reduces the effectiveness of training and increases the risk of injury.

Common injuries in rugby

Dislocations

A dislocation occurs when bones at a joint (articulating bones) are separated as a result of the joint being forced beyond its normal range of movement. All joints can be dislocated, fingers being the joint most commonly dislocated in rugby. All dislocations should be approached with caution and treated by appropriate medical staff.

Dislocated shoulder

The shoulder is a ball and socket joint and is capable of a great deal of movement. However, it is not a particularly stable joint because of the shallowness of the socket, which makes it more susceptible to dislocation. Once the joint has been dislocated it will be more prone to reoccurrence (especially if it occurs below the age of 25) as the elasticity of the ligaments and tendons has been increased, which further reduces the stability of the shoulder.

When the arm is moved away from the body (abducted) and the shoulder is rotated outwards, the joint is particularly vulnerable. In this position, if any great/fast force is applied then the upper arm bone (humerus) can be forced out of the socket. This is a full dislocation and is termed 'anterior' when the humerus pops out to the front (most common), or 'posterior' when the humerus pops out at the back.

The shoulder can also suffer from subluxation, which is when the humerus comes out of the socket but immediately goes back into place. This is fairly common in loose-jointed people and those who have suffered a number of dislocations.

In rugby these injuries occur commonly while tackling or through contact with the ground.

Treatment

You should never try to replace a dislocation yourself as there is the risk of causing further damage to the muscles, ligaments and nerves around the joint. Players should be seen by a doctor as soon as possible to have the dislocation corrected. This generally means a trip to your local A and E so an X-ray can be taken to rule out a fracture and check the position of the head of the humerus.

Recovery time

The arm will be in a sling for two to three weeks and no overhead work should be carried out for six weeks, although active recovery work should begin as soon as possible. Surgery may be required to restabilise the joint and to reduce the chance of further dislocation.

Preventative strategy

Carrying out proprioception, stabilisation work and strengthening the shoulder and scapular region will help to reduce the chance of dislocation and injury. Some examples are given below.

Theraband resistance

Rotator cuff medial rotation using a theraband for resistance in the dislocation range will help to stabilise the joint. Grip the theraband with the arm abducted, elevated and laterally rotated, pull down and return to the start position with control.

Stability push-ups

Perform push-ups against a wall using a Swiss ball to provide instability. Alternatively, perform push-ups with both hands on a wobble board or medicine ball, progressing to one hand on the ball and one on the ground. These exercises will develop the muscles of the rotator cuff and general shoulder stability.

Shoulder step-ups

Step the hands up and down in turn to complete one repetition of the exercise, keeping the core stable by drawing in throughout the exercise. Perform between 5 and 10 step-ups for each side and 2–3 sets with 1–2 minutes recovery between. This again works and develops the shoulder stabilisers.

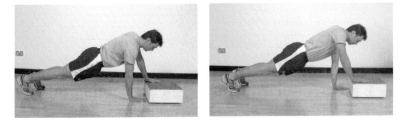

Acromioclavicular joint (ACjt) dislocation

This is a very common rugby injury, usually occurring from a fall onto the side. Sometimes the clavicle (collar bone) will break but if it doesn't the ACjt will be disrupted and will cause pain. This subluxation/dislocation will need to be seen by a doctor or physiotherapist and commonly leaves a bump on the top of the shoulder.

There are other muscular injuries around the shoulder from muscle imbalances that cause pain and impingements. These should all be seen by a doctor/physiotherapist and it is important the player does not continue playing or training without assessment.

Muscular injuries

A muscle is damaged when it is forcibly stretched (pulled) beyond its usual limit of movement; the muscle tissue is torn, resulting in bleeding in the tissue that can last up to 72 hours. There are various degrees of strain, which are classified based on their severity.

Table 11.1 Classification of strains

Strain	Damage to muscle	Symptoms	Approximate recovery time
Unclassified	Less than 5 per cent of fibres torn	Slight tenderness	5 days
1st degree	Less than 25 per cent of fibres torn	Tender but no impairment of muscle action	3 weeks
2nd degree	25–75 per cent of fibres torn	Swelling, bruising and some limitation of mobility	4–6 weeks
3rd degree	Complete rupture of fibres within the muscle (torn in two)	Extreme tenderness, severe bruising and impairment of movement	12 weeks and often requires surgery

The recovery times in table 11.1 are only approximate; other factors must be taken into account when using these guidelines. Continuing to play with the injury, if it is a recurring injury, and drinking alcohol after the injury will all influence the recovery time and treatment.

Hamstring

The most commonly injured muscle in rugby is the hamstring, which is made up of three muscles (bicep femoris, semitendinosus and semimembranosus) whose function is to bend the knee and extend the hip. Sprinting, stopping, jumping and kicking actions are the most common cause of hamstring injuries and players are most vulnerable to this when they are fatigued.

Treatment
As with all muscular injuries the RICE protocol should be followed:

R	rest
I	ice
C	compression
E	elevation

Do not compress and elevate at the same time as this can result in tissue damage, as the excessively reduced flow of blood starves the muscle of oxygen.

Icing, compression and elevation help to reduce the bleeding and damage within the muscle, thus speeding up recovery time. Players often ignore the rest element, but if ignored it can result in an increase in the degree of injury.

Icing should take place with the muscle in an elevated position for 10 minutes every two hours for the first two days. The ice should never be applied directly to the skin (apply through a clean wet cloth to avoid ice burns). Ice is more effective than chemical ice packs as they can initially get too cold, causing a burn, and then lose their coldness much more quickly than ice does. Applying ice for longer than this actually increases the swelling as the body augments the blood flow to warm the area.

Ice massage (stroking movement with ice pack) can take place after three days and can last for over 10 minutes. This causes the blood vessels to dilate and constrict, alternately increasing and decreasing the blood flow to the area, and therefore bringing nutrients to help the healing process. Sometimes ice bathing can be useful, but this should only be done under the supervision of a physiotherapist as prolonged icing to areas with little subcutaneous fat can affect the superficial nerves. After three to five days of rest an active recovery programme can be undertaken with stretching of the muscle to lengthen the scar tissue and increase muscle strength.

Scar tissue – bleeding takes place when a muscle is torn, and this blood fills the gap between the torn muscle ends. This forms a link between the two ends and anchors them together, forming scar tissue that makes the muscle more resistant to stretching. The muscle shortens as a result and, if progressive mobilisation is not conducted, the muscle will be more likely to tear again.

Preventative strategy

Preventing muscle injuries is largely dependent upon an appropriate warm-up and dynamic stretching programme with the sport-specific actions mimicked in this process. An appropriate cool-down to remove waste products should also be conducted. Following a functional strength training programme will also reduce the chance of muscular injury.

A flexibility programme is a must for all athletes, as developing the range of motion (ROM) that muscles can function at will reduce the likelihood of strains occurring. This should be a separate training session whose sole aim is to improve ROM at the joints.

Cramp

Though this is not an injury, it is a condition that affects a number of players and is worthy of further discussion in this chapter. Cramp is the sudden and involuntary contraction of a muscle (or part of a muscle) that does not then immediately relax. This can be a very painful experience that makes it very difficult for the player to continue playing, as he/she will be unable to control the function of this muscle.

The calf is the muscle that is most frequently affected; the hamstring, quadricep, feet and hands are also prone to cramping. Cramp can be caused by a number of factors:

- poor flexibility
- fatigue
- dehydration and electrolyte depletion
- heat
- pitch conditions
- injury
- general fitness levels.

Preventative strategy

A good level of fitness will reduce the likelihood of cramp as there will be an improved blood supply carrying oxygen and minerals to the muscles. While developing flexibility and stretching muscles before activity will help to reduce muscle tightness, players who are prone to cramp should spend more time stretching and preparing these muscles for exercise. Ensuring the body is properly hydrated is critical in preventing cramp and players need to develop a hydration strategy before, during and after the game.

Treatment

If you suffer an attack of cramp, you should immediately cease the activity you were doing – if you have a severe case, you will have little choice but to do so. Gently stretch the muscle or muscle group and attempt to promote blood flow with light massage to provide heat. When possible, begin to move the affected muscles and continue to rehydrate to replace fluid, minerals and electrolytes.

Sprains

A sprain is an injury to a ligament, and is usually caused by a sudden forceful movement taking the joint beyond its normal range of motion, but not necessarily resulting in a dislocation. As with strains, sprains are classified based on the severity of the injury.

Table 11.2 Classification of sprains

Sprain	Damage	Symptoms	Approximate recovery time
1st degree	Minimal	Mild tenderness, slight swelling but no or very little loss of movement at joint and no joint instability	2–4 weeks depending on ligament and joint injured
2nd degree	Ligament may become partially detached	Swelling, bruising, localised tenderness, moderate pain and some loss of joint mobility, but little to no joint instability	3–12 weeks depending on ligament and joint injured
3rd degree	Complete rupture of ligament fibres torn in two or separated from the bone	Swelling, variable pain and extreme joint instability	3–10 months depending on ligament and joint injured; may require surgery

The multi-directional and contact nature of rugby means that the body is continually having great force placed upon it. These forces and the angles that are applied to the body are the reason for the majority of ligament injuries that occur in rugby.

The ankle, shoulder and knee are all placed under extreme forces throughout a game of rugby and it is these joints that most commonly suffer ligament damage. The ankle commonly suffers an inversion sprain when a player 'goes over on the ankle', pushing the foot down and in.

There are many types of injury that can occur at the knee, the most famous and serious being the anterior cruciate ligament (ACL). This can occur if the foot is planted in the ground when the tackle is made, twisting the knee inwards. An ACL injury will often also result in damage to the medial collateral ligament (MCL) and medial cartilage on the inside of the knee, and is the most commonly injured knee ligament. Injury to this ligament usually occurs as the result of an impact on the outside of the knee that forces the knee joint in towards the opposite knee.

Treatment

Sprains should be treated under the RICE principle. Diagnosis can be difficult in the early stage due to swelling, so the injury should be assessed by a physiotherapist/doctor and an appropriate rest and recovery programme planned.

Preventative strategy

Joints can be made less vulnerable to damage by carrying out appropriate proprioception, stabilisation and functional weight training. This training will help to prepare the joints for the forces they will encounter in a game and help them to function more effectively, individually and collectively.

Proprioception – sensory receptors in the muscles, tendons and joints provide information about the position and state of muscle contraction and joints. This information is then used by the central nervous system (CNS) to produce controlled and co-ordinated movement.

Practising on wobble boards and jelly discs helps to heighten these senses and prepares the muscles for working in the unstable positions that occur in rugby. Such practice will improve balance, muscle co-ordination and sensory proprioception and will reduce the risk of injury. Closing your eyes when performing proprioception exercises increases the difficulty level as visual cues for the CNS are removed.

ACL and MCL sprains

Strong hamstring and quadriceps muscles are a major factor in reducing the risk of an ACL or MCL strain. Squats, lunges, straight and single-leg dead lifts and Swiss ball leg curls are all exercises that a player should utilise for this end. In order to prevent damage to the knee joint, players need to practise landing with a soft contact and bent knees to reduce the force being transmitted through the knee joint. The same principles apply with changing direction and stepping practices.

The exercises below will help to strengthen the knee and ankle joints, bring about greater multi-joint co-ordination and improve movement patterns. It will also bring about improvements in balance and muscle reaction time, allowing for more powerful movements and reducing the chance of injury.

Squatting

Use an unstable surface such as jelly discs or wobble boards. This can be progressed to one-legged squats or squats with the eyes closed to increase the difficulty.

Alternatively, squat with a Swiss ball between your back and a wall, with your thighs parallel to the ground; hold the squat position, squeeze a ball or foam pad between your knees and pull your toes up towards your face. Hold for 5–10 seconds and repeat after a short rest. This works the quadriceps and gluteus muscles, helps to prevent patellar pain and maintains the alignment of the knee. Pulling the toes up works the muscles around the shin and will also help reduce the risk of shin splints.

Calf raise

Perform the exercise on a jelly disc or wobble board to increase the need for stability around the ankle joint. The calf raise can also be performed with a band providing resistance and again increasing the degree to which the ankle stabilisers are activated.

Alternatively, elevate one leg on a box and push against the resistance of a band to the side. Then resist against the pull of the band at this point for five seconds. Return to the start position, repeat this three times and then work the opposite leg. This will develop the muscles on the outside of the ankle and help to reduce the risk of sprains.

Shin splints

Shin splints are quite common in rugby, especially in the pre-season phase of training, when the ground is hard and the amount of running is at its greatest. Shin splints are commonly used to describe a number of overuse injuries situated on the inside or outside of the shin bone (tibia), and are associated with a dull aching pain that is brought on by exercise but goes away when exercise is ceased.

Shin splints can be caused by a direct blow, incorrect running technique, poor footwear, pronation of feet (rolling inwards), muscle imbalance, training on hard surfaces and, most commonly, an increase in the intensity and frequency of exercise, generally running.

Shin splints should be treated following the RICE principle, with rest, anti-inflammatory medication, stretching, self-massage and strengthening exercises to help reduce the pressure.

Preventative strategy

To reduce the chance of suffering from shin splints you need to ensure that the muscles in the shin that control flexion at the ankle are strengthened. It is a weakness in these muscles that results in the foot landing with excessive force, which brings on shin-splint injuries.

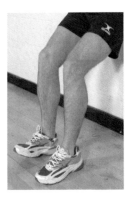

Shin raise

Rest your shoulders and back against a wall and, keeping your heels on the floor, bring your toes up towards your shin. Lower your feet down but do not let your toes touch the floor; repeat this 15 times.

Exercise and illness

Common sense would tell you that to train when ill is something that should be avoided, as the body is not functioning in its normal state and exercise will most likely delay the return to normal. As a result of this, the workout will be below your normal training level and no gains will be made from training; however, many athletes find it difficult both mentally and physically not to train when a session has been planned and will perform the session regardless.

If the symptoms of the illness are above the neck – runny or stuffy nose, sneezing, watery eyes or sore throat – then you can start to train at about half your normal workout intensity. If after 10–15 minutes of exercise you feel better, then increase the intensity and carry on the workout as normal. If you feel no better, you should stop training and replenish the body's vitamin C levels, ensure hydration levels are maintained and rest a day or two before resuming training.

If the symptoms of your illness are below the neck – aching muscles, hacking cough, nausea and vomiting or diarrhoea – then you should not train as doing so will delay recovery. Never train when suffering from flu or if you have a virus, as this places extra strain on the heart muscle.

Injury management/prevention and LTAD

FUNdamental (6–8 years) and learning to train (9–11 years)

Due to the nature and intensity of the activity recommended at these stages, the injuries sustained will generally be the cuts and bruises associated with young people and activity.

Training to train (12–14 years)

From this point on there is more opportunity to play matches, more contact situations and more players on the pitch, so the risk of injury is increased. It is recommended that from this stage on only one match is played per week, with the emphasis being on physical and technical preparation in order to maximise the training windows of opportunity.

Training to compete (15–17 years), learning to win and training to win (18 years+)

The increase in intensity and type of training in the later stages of the LTAD pathway often result in players carrying injuries. It is vital that appropriate rest and recovery time is included in any programme and that preventative and rehabilitation work is carried out to ensure the risk of injury is minimised.

Visit www.rfu.com to download a copy of the youth structured season to help you plan the playing and training requirements for your team.

Summary

A large proportion of injuries are actually old injuries that are reoccurring. This indicates that athletes are not managing the injury correctly or ensuring that the appropriate recovery and strengthening of the affected area is taking place. Rest and ice tend to allow athletes to resume the activity that caused the injury without actually bringing about any improvements to the affected area; therefore, it is little surprise that injury reoccurs.

In the event of a player sustaining an injury, an appropriate recovery and strengthening programme must be devised under the guidance of a physiotherapist. Only after this has been conducted and an appropriate rugby-specific fitness test has taken place should a player be cleared to return to playing. It is also important to deal with the psychological effects of being unable to play and to ensure the player retains a positive focus.

The preventative strategies and methods discussed in this chapter will not guarantee that your players will not sustain injuries, but they will reduce the likelihood of such an occurrence. Any preventative strategy should be implemented in consultation with the club physiotherapist and after an appropriate assessment of the player has been carried out. These exercises can be carried out as part of a strength session or as a specific preventative session. Including them in players' day-to-day training does make them more easily accepted and thus more likely to be performed than if prescribed as a stand-alone session.

Bibliography

Anderson, O. (2004), 'The Best Exercises to Recover from the Most Frequent Sports Injuries', *Sports Injury Bulletin*, 2004, pp. 1–12.

Anderson, O. (2004), 'Can Proper Proprioception Training Reduce Your Probability of Injury?' *Sports Injury Bulletin*, March 2002, pp. 1–8.

Anson, P. (2003), 'Rugby Specific Speed Work', *RFU Technical Journal*, Autumn 2003, pp. 33–4.

Baechle, T. and Earle, R. (2000), *Essentials of Strength Training and Conditioning*, Human Kinetics, Champaign, Ill.

Bayli, I. (2002), *Long Term Athlete Development, System Building, Alignment and Integration*, Sport England – LTAD Workshops.

Bean, A. (2003), *The Complete Guide to Sports Nutrition*, 4th Edition, A & C Black, London.

Beaulieu, J. E. (1981), 'Developing a stretching programme', *Physician Sports Medicine*, 9(11), pp. 59–65.

Bento, D. (2001), 'Sprint Running Needs of Field Sport Athletes: A New Perspective', *Sports Coach*, 24(2), pp. 12–14.

Boyle, M (2004), *Functional Training for Sport*, Human Kinetics, Champaign, Ill.

Brandon, R. (2002), 'Injury Prevention', *Sports Injury Bulletin*, April 2002, pp. 8–10.

Brandon, R. (2003), 'How Rugby Players Should Train to Reflect the Varying Energy Demands on Their Field Positions', *Peak Performance*, No. 185, pp. 4–6.

Brewer, C (2002), 'Structuring the Training Year', *RFU Technical Journal*, Summer 2002, pp. 23–7.

Brewer, C. (2002), 'The Big 5 Lifts for Rugby Union Players', *RFU Technical Journal*, Spring 2002, pp. 34–40.

Broad, N. (2004), 'Nutrition: The Premiership Approach to Science', *Peak Performance*, April 2004 No. 196, pp. 1–4.

Buckingham, M. (2000), *Core Stability and Balance in the Body*, RFU National Coaching Development Resource Library.

Carlton, I. (2004), 'Nutrition: Can Fat Challenge Carbs as a Performance Aid?' *Peak Performance*, June 2004, No. 182, pp. 7–10.

Casajus, J. (2003), 'Determination of work rates in rugby', Presentation at the

International Conference on the Science and Practice of Rugby, November 2003, Brisbane.

Clarkson, M. (1999), *Competitive Fire*, Human Kinetics, Champaign, Ill.

Club England Fitness Team (2000), *Strength Training and the Young Rugby Player*, RFU National Coaching Development Resource Library.

Cox, R. (2003), 'Nutrient Intake and Timing Key to Building Lean Muscle', ACSM *Fit Society Page*, Fall 2003, p. 3.

Crust, L. (2004), 'The Majestic Self-Confidence of Jonny Wilkinson', *Peak Performance*, No. 191, pp. 1–4.

Crust, L. (2004), 'Mental Toughness', *Peak Performance*, No. 185, pp. 1–4.

Crust, L. (2004) 'Performance Profiling', *Peak Performance*, No. 183, pp. 7–9.

Crust, L. (2003), 'For Peak Experiences in Sport, You Need to Go With The Flow', *Peak Performance*, No. 182, pp. 3–6.

Delavier, F. (2001), *Strength Training Anatomy*, Human Kinetics, Champaign, Ill.

De Vries, H.A. (1986), 'Physiology of Flexibility', *Physiology of Exercise for PE and Athletics*, pp. 462–71.

Dickinson, P. (2000), *Power Play*, RFU National Coaching Development Resource Library.

Ekstrand. (1982), 'Lower Extremity Measurements', *Physiology Medical Rehabilitation*, 63, pp. 171–5.

Foran, B. (ed.) (2001), *High Performance Sports Conditioning*, Human Kinetics, Champaign, Ill.

Hale, B. and Collins, D. (2002), *Rugby Tough*, Human Kinetics, Champaign, Ill.

Hamilton, A. (2003), 'Essential Fats are the Answer to Most Athletes Prayers: Helping Your Body to Conserve Carbohydrate While Shedding Fat', *Peak Performance*, December 2003, No. 190, pp 1–4.

Hazeldine, R. and McNab, T. (1998), *The RFU Guide to Fitness for Rugby*, A & C Black, London.

Holland, G. J. (1949), 'Physiology of Flexibility', *Kinesiology Review*.

Humphrey, L. D. (1981), 'Flexibility', *Journal of Physical Education and Recreation*, 52, pp. 41–3.

IRB (2004), *Laws of the Game – Rugby Union 2004*, Dublin, IRB.

Kent, M. (1998), *The Oxford Dictionary of Sports Science*, OUP, Oxford.

Kinakin, K. (2004), *Optimal Muscle Training*, Human Kinetics, Champaign, Ill.

Larsen, U. (2004), 'Pilates: Clinical Execution', *Sports Injury Bulletin*, October 2004, No. 43, pp. 1–7.

Larsen, U. (2004), 'Pilates Under Pressure', *Sports Injury Bulletin*, September 2004, No. 42, pp. 1–4.

Maughan, R. (2004), 'How Athletes Can Benefit From World Consensus on Sport Nutrition', *Peak Performance*, February 2004, No. 193, pp. 5–6.

Maughan, R. (2004), 'Nutrition: It Used to be Oranges in the Centre Circle... Now It's Personal Hydration Strategy', *Peak Performance*, April 2004, No. 196, pp. 6–7.

Noakes, T. (1991), *The Lore of Running*, Human Kinetics, Champaign, Ill.

Pearson, A. (2001), *Speed, Agility and Quickness for Rugby*, A & C Black, London.

Powers, S. and Howley, T. (2001), *Exercise Physiology*, McGraw-Hill, New York.

Radcliffe, J. and Farentinos, R. (1999), *High Powered Plyometrics*, Human Kinetics, Champaign, Ill.

Reddin, D. (2000), 'The Physiological Background to Weights Based Power Training', RFU National Coaching Development Resource Library.

Reddin, D. (1998), 'England Rugby – Fitness Testing', *RFU Technical Journal*, Winter 1998/99, pp. 28–29.

Reddin, D., Carey, A. and Lovell, M. (2003), *Nutritional Guidelines for England Players and Coaches*, RFU.

Reddin, D. and Morris, C. (2002), *Academy Fitness Test Protocols*, RFU, Twickenham.

RFU (2004), *Long Term Athlete Development: Developing Future World Class Pathways of Long Term Rugby Excellence*, RFU, Twickenham.

Shepherd, J. (2004), 'Building Rotational Power', *Peak Performance*, May 2004, No. 197, pp. 4–6.

Shepherd, J. (2004), 'Speed: How Sprinters Can Train Smart to Maintain Their Quicksilver Qualities', *Peak Performance*, January 2004, No. 192, pp. 1–3.

Shyne, K. and Dominguez, H. (1982), 'To stretch or not to stretch', *Physician Sports Medicine*, 10(9), pp. 137–40.

The Football Association Medical and Sports Science Department, (2001), *F.A. Fitness Trainers Award Pre-Course Introduction*, Part 2, F.A., Lilleshall.

Thomas, C (2003), 'IRB Game Analysis – Part 1', *RFU Technical Journal*, Autumn 2003, pp. 24–27.

Wilmore, N and Costill D (1994), *Physiology of Sports and Exercise*, Human Kinetics, Champaign Ill.

Wilmore, J. (1993), 'Body Composition in Sport and Exercise: Directions for Future Research', *Medical Science and Sports Exercise Journal*, 15, pp. 21–31.

Yakovlev, N. (1967), 'Sports Biochemistry', DHFK, Leipzig.

Web-based sources

www.acsm.org
The American College of Sports Medicine is a leading researcher in the world of sport and health, and has an extensive library of resources on a wide range of sporting issues.

www.brianmac.demon.co.uk
This site contains recent research articles on a wide range of subjects, and has an excellent section on fitness testing and how to ensure reliability and validity of results.

www.disen.org
A great deal of excellent information regarding nutrition in sport is found at this site, which also has up-to-date research and publications that can be purchased.

www.insitefitness.com.au
From here you can link into a variety of sites to access research articles, and general fitness information is contained within the site itself.

www.fitness4rugby.com
This site provides rugby-specific fitness advice as well as a shopping facility where you can purchase books and equipment.

www.mendosa.com
This site contains a great deal of information on diabetes, general nutritional advice and the components of a healthy diet.

www.physioroom.com
A site widely used by physiotherapists for up-to-date research on treatments and injury prevention. Very user-friendly for athletes and coaches attempting to gain a basic understanding of preventative strategies and treatments.

www.scrum.com
This website provides excellent practical advice on fitness for rugby from noted experts such as Clive Brewer.

www.sportsci.org
This site contains a reference base of articles published by leading researchers.

Index